SEVEN SPRINGS COUNTRY CLUB

A Century of Stewardship

MaryEllen Reardon

Amazon KDP

Copyright © 2022 KDP

All rights reserved

The characters and events portrayed in this book are fictitious. Any similarity to real persons, living or dead, is coincidental and not intended by the author.

No part of this book may be reproduced, or stored in a retrieval system, or transmitted in any form or by any means, electronic, mechanical, photocopying, recording, or otherwise, without express written permission of the publisher.

ISBN-13: 9798781636006
ISBN-10: 1477123456

Cover design by: Tom Kowal
Library of Congress Control Number: 2018675309
Printed in the United States of America

To my parents, James and Kathleen McGee for introducing me to Seven Springs.

To Jason, James, Thomas, and Sean for making it a home.

A huge debt of gratitude is owed to Donna Kowal for her immense help editing this project.
Thank you to Tom Kowal for his cover art and tireless photo editing

Thank you to Ed Ferris, Mary Carver and Maddie Ferris for their personal memories, photos and invaluable knowledge of Seven Springs history.
Thank you to Wayne Younge for his research assistance.
Thank you to John Bertrand and Marilyn Rabenhorst for sharing their stories of the Mason and Russell families.

Birds for the air, fish for the water and me for the woods - and I for the woods

                                                EDWARD RUSSELL, 1928

CONTENTS

Title Page
Copyright
Dedication
Dedication
Epigraph
Section I   1
Chapter 1   2
Chapter 2   4
Section II   6
Chapter 3   7
Charter Members of Seven Springs Country Club   10
Section III   11
Chapter 4   12
Chapter 5   14
Chapter 6   16
Chapter 7   19
Section IV   22
Chapter 8   23
Chapter 9   26
Chapter 10   28

Chapter 11	30
The Bridge Builder	32
Section V	33
Chapter 12	34
Chapter 13	37
Chapter 14	40
Section VI	45
Section VII	60
Chapter 15	61
Chapter 16	64
Section VIII	66
Chapter 17	67
Chapter 18	70
Chapter 19	72
Chapter 20	74
Chapter 21	76
Chapter 22	78
Chapter 23	80
Chapter 24	82
Chapter 25	84
Chapter 26	86
Chapter 27	87
Chapter 28	89
Chapter 29	91
Chapter 30	93
Chapter 31	95
Chapter 32	97
Chapter 33	99

Chapter 34	101
Chapter 35	103
Chapter 36	105
Chapter 37	106
Chapter 38	108
Chapter 39	110
Chapter 40	112
Chapter 41	113
Section IX	115
Chapter 42	118
Chapter 43	121
References	129
Epilogue	141
Contact	143
About The Author	145

SECTION I

History

CHAPTER 1
The Place of the Clear Running Water

Seven Springs has long been a special place. While those who live here and visit know of its peacefulness and beauty, this was recognized long before the founding of the Country Club. Before the European settlers arrived, Seven Springs, along with all of Western New York, was where the Haudenosaunee resided.

The following passage is courtesy of the Rochester Zen Center. It is a retelling of an oral history of Native American people in Western New York.

There is a place in western New York State that has been special to many peoples for several hundred years. Prior to 1809 this area was a crossroads, a stopping place for rest and replenishment for peoples of the Iroquois Nation, Mohawk, Seneca and Tonawanda, a place of peace. It was called "The Place of Clear Running Waters" because of the numerous springs that fed the stream which flowed into ponds that sustained fish, flora, and fauna. While in this area tribal disputes, animosities and rivalries were set aside as no blood was to be shed, the waters were to remain clear. Dutch fur traders settled in the area; towns flourished and the woodland paths that the Native Americans walked became roads.

The place of Clear Running Waters was seen as ideal for the first grist mill in the county, and so it was. In 1809 the stream was diverted and diked to create a pond, using the surrounding trees as the foundation. The grist mill with its undershot wheel was built in 1811 from the resources of the land: stone and timber. Grist was ground there for 80 years before the water wheel was disengaged from the millstones. A house had been built and a parson lived there for a time. A man named Gardner bought the property and built a barn and outbuildings. It was now called Gardner's Pond. The Native Americans had gone or had been sent elsewhere.

The passage continues on to include more modern history

In the first quarter of the 20th century the place was purchased by the Gubb family, who were respectful and honored the land. It was used as a riding camp and stables in the warm summer months, with brindle paths throughout the woods, swimming in the pond, children laughing - happy energy. In 1948 the Chapin family bought the land from their cousins, and they lived there for over 50 years, cherishing, and nurturing its intrinsic peace and sacredness. To honor and preserve the sacredness of this land, the family has given it to a Buddhist community to build a retreat facility and training center for Zen Buddhist practice.

Although this story highlights the neighboring property of Chapin Mill, is important to understand that Seven Springs has been part of a place of peace and plenty for so long. We hope it will continue this way for generations to come.

"A Short History of Chapin Mill "Courtesy of the Rochester Zen Center, as told to Andris Chapin by Avis Sundown Sky, a clan mother of the Tonawanda tribe.

CHAPTER 2
The Early Days

Genesee County and the town of Batavia were founded in 1802 and the town of Stafford in 1820. However, the settlement of the area began before that, when the Big Tree Treaty with the Seneca allowed for the development of settlements in the Western New York area.

In conducting research, it was difficult to follow the line of landowners. An article written about Horseshoe Lake gave the following information about the early days. "In 1804, John Debow and Zenas Bigelow began the cultivation of land in Stafford.", This is where Bigelow Creek got its name. The article goes on to say that in 1811 a sawmill was built by Amos Stow on Bigelow Creek and a grist mill was built by Seymour Ensign on his pond, which later became known as Gardner's Pond and today is part of the Chapin Mill Retreat Center. In addition to the grist mill, Mr. Ensign also had a business carding wool and cloth dressing.

According to an early gazetteer of Genesee County, Mr. Ensign settled in Batavia in 1809. However, the records do not confirm that Mr. Ensign was the first property owner in the area encompassing Seven Springs and The Chapin Mill Retreat Center. That said, there is a good amount of information about the early days of the Club.

SECTION II

The Formation of Seven Springs

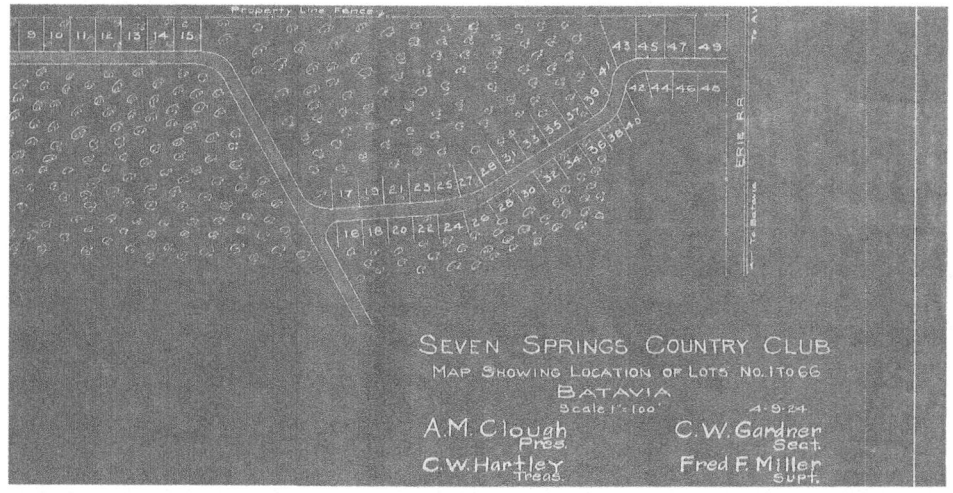

CHAPTER 3
The Formation of Seven Springs

William "Billy" Russell purchased a tract of 55 acres on the border between Batavia and Stafford in 1910. It was an area that his father, Edward Russell had long admired. An additional two and a half acres were soon purchased from nearby farmer Jerome Whittleton. It was at that same time when a group of businessmen and members of the Genesee County Fish and Game Association came together to form Seven Springs Country Club. The Club was established to be a place of recreation and enjoyment for its members. No hunting was allowed within the Club grounds, but members were able to fish. The organization of Seven Springs began to take form with 28 charter members in 1910. In December of that year with Club approval, a mortgage was written between William Russell and Mrs. Cora Griswold North in the amount of $1500.00 at 5% for a period of five years.

A 1911 article announcing the formation of the Club described the property by saying "The location is an ideal one and is one of the most beautiful wild spots in Genesee County".

Articles of Incorporation were also issued by the Secretary of State in 1911. The Club was formed in order to "establish and maintain a country club for intellectual improvement, social intercourse, sport and recreation". In March of that year Edward Russell was named the first President, C.A. Willyoung as the treasurer, and JB Jones was named as the Secretary. A Board of Directors was also created with nine members. The Club was capitalized at $5000 with 50 shares at $100 each. Documentation from 1911 noted 48 members with dues of $5 annually. At first, membership in Seven Springs was limited to 50 members but that was increased to 100 by the end of 1911.

Edward Russell and Cleve Gillette set up camp and spent the winter of 1911 living on the property in a tent. Mr. Russell was quoted as saying they were protected from the cold and wind because their tent was placed in a hollow. He said they had enough supplies and firewood, and water was taken right from the spring. They spent the winter cutting down old growth and clearing land for the proposed lake and dam. For these difficult tasks they were each paid a wage of two dollars a day. The article was written in January of 1912 and stated that Mr. Russell expected to return to his own home on West Main Street soon. He did go on to build a cottage in those first couple of years and used it when he was staying in the Springs. It was known as the "Caretakers Cottage" and today it is known as "The Yellow Cottage" at the head of the lake.

In 1912, the dam was completed, and the five-acre lake was formed. Trees planted the first year did not do well and so more were planted in 1913. These trees grew and thrived. From that time on new trees were planted every year. In August of 1912, the property was visited by former State Fish and Game Commissioner, J.S. Whipple. In the *Batavia Daily News*, he was quoted as saying "I do not believe you fully realize what a valuable and rare piece of property you have here. It is like a section of the Adirondacks without their discomforts".

By 1914 cottages were beginning to be built by members. The cottages were small, consisting of one or two rooms. They did not have running water or electricity and were used mostly as summer retreats.

In the early part of the 20th century people began to understand the importance of protecting and replacing natural resources. Seven Springs is unique in that it was designed to do just that. The founders were both businessmen of means and members of the Fish and Game Association. Their purpose in building the Club was to turn mostly bare land and turn it into beautiful, lush woods to be enjoyed for generations to come.

CHARTER MEMBERS OF SEVEN SPRINGS COUNTRY CLUB

1911

M.C. Bergman
John Brown
William Casey
Ralph Crickler
Richard Delaney
Henry Dewolf
C.S. Dewolf
Frank Ebling
Thomas Gallagher
Cleve Gillette
George Glade
J. Edward Gubb
Charles Hartley
Arthur Hough
Dr. William Johnson
K.B. Mathes
Charles Pixley
Jay L. Robson
Edward Russell
William Russell
J.W. Totterdale
Howard Tyler
Melvin J. Tyler
Frank C. Walker
Judge E. Washburn
George Watson
Charles A. Williams
C.A. Willyoung

SECTION III

Seven Springs Founders

CHAPTER 4
The Canty Family

Thomas Canty was born in Canada in 1876 to William and Mary Canty. He had a twin brother named Arthur along with siblings May, Alice, Henry, and Sadie. According to census records, the family moved to the U.S. in 1880 and by 1900 the family lived in Batavia, Thomas was an employee of the PW Minor shoe factory where he worked for many years.

In 1903 Thomas was married to Anna Green and they began their family. The wedding announcement stated that the couple were "well-known and popular young people". Thomas and Anna made their home on Manhattan Avenue in Batavia and went on to raise seven children: Thomas Jr, William, Rose, Daniel, Mary, John, and Anna Mae.

Thomas joined Seven Springs and became a cottage owner in 1915. The original cottage burned down in 1935 and was rebuilt by Thomas. (Cottage #10). The Canty family enjoyed the cottage for many years. Long after Anna died in 1953 and Thomas in 1969, the family continued to be a mainstay of the Springs community.

Daniel took over the Canty cottage in 1969 after his father's death that same year. Daniel married Frances Powers and they had four children. Daniel's name came up in newspaper articles following an accident. When he was 16, he was working as a caddie at Stafford Country Club when he was hit by a golf club. Daniel suffered a serious injury to one of his eyes, it was feared that he would lose his sight in one eye. He made a full recovery and later died in 1991.

As for Daniel's siblings, Thomas Jr. graduated from the University of Notre Dame, and also studied at New York University. He worked in the insurance industry, and records show that he married twice and had a daughter. Thomas Jr. died in 1967. William became a project engineer with the railroad and lived in Batavia. He was married to Leona and had two children Richard and Barbara. William died in Batavia in 1977. John, who went by J. Edward, was the President of the H.E. Turner Funeral Home. He married Marie Townsend and they had a daughter. He died in 1993

The oldest sister, Rose, passed away in 1926 at the young age of 18. There was mention of Rose being seriously ill in a Batavia newspaper, but no further information was found. Mary married Clarence Majerus, and they raised a family together. Mary died in 1994. Lastly, born on September 13, 1917, Anna Mae was the youngest of the Canty children. Anna Mae was a nurse. She married Leonard Balling and they made their home in North Tonawanda. She was the mother of Bernard, Thomas, Deborah, Kenneth, William, Joan, Jean, and Lenore. Upon her husband's death, Anna Mae purchased Cottage #20 (The Pink Candle) in 1976, and, when she died in 2004, her daughter Joan Post became the owner. Also, Anna Mae's daughter Deborah became a Club member, and her sons Ken and Billy became the owners of their grandfather's cottage (Cottage #10), which was later passed on to Billy's son, Cody.

CHAPTER 5
Ernie Hawkins

Ernie Hawkins proved to be the most difficult of the Club members to research. Known in Seven Springs as Ernie, he was also found under the name Stuart. Depending on the census, he was sometimes listed as Ernest and at other times he was listed as Stuart. In a wedding announcement for his niece, his name appeared as Ernest Stuart Hawkins. Ernie served as a long-time President of Seven Springs. In the words of a member who knew him "Whatever Ernie said, was the way it went".

Ernie was born in Warsaw, NY in 1915, the only son of Harry J and Ida Hunter Hawkins. His father Harry was born in England and came to the U.S. in 1887. His mother Ida was born in Ontario, Canada and came to the U.S. in approximately 1890. Both of his parents became naturalized citizens. Ernie had four sisters: Mildred, Caroline, Evelyn, and Phyllis. The family moved to Batavia, where their father, John, who was a machinist, owned his own garage.

Ernie was an athlete; he was quite tall and played basketball throughout high school. It appears that he followed his father's footsteps in the automobile business. The 1940 census noted he was married to Frances, and they had a daughter named Patricia. He reported his occupation as working in wholesale automobile accessories.

As life circumstances changed, in the mid 1940's, Ernie married Ethel Persons Bussing, and she had a daughter named Naomi from her first marriage. Ernie became a Seven Springs member in 1944. By the following year, Ernie and his wife Ethel were living at Cottage #17 (currently owned by the Rapones). Ernie devoted many years to supporting Seven Springs, and the Club grew and thrived under his guidance. When Ernie died in 1982 Ethel sold their cottage to Bob Crook and moved to Salt Lake City to live with her daughter. She married one more time and died in 2005. Today the cottage stands on the road that bears his name.

While researching Seven Spring history, one common theme is that many members are connected to each other. Ernie Hawkins and his family are good examples of this. On the 1930 census Ernie, his parents and siblings lived on Trumbull Parkway in Batavia. Their next-door neighbors were Vernon and Florence Carnahan. Vern and his brother Gordon both became Seven Springs cottage owners. Ernie's sister, Evelyn married Alfred Gover and the couple were also members and cottage owners (present day Kohorst's cottage). Ernie's niece was Carol Zillman, along with her husband Rex also owned a cottage in the Springs (present day Reardon's). Ernie was also connected to the O'Brien family- he was the uncle of current member Betty Hawkins O'Brien

CHAPTER 6
Fred Miller

Fred Miller was a well-known man, not only in Seven Springs but throughout Western New York. He was called the "Sage of Seven Springs" and was well regarded for his ability to predict the weather-not to mention his knack for feeding a crowd.

He was born in Lyons, N.Y. on March 7, 1863, to parents George and Magalena Roessel Miller. Both of his parents were born in Lembach, Bas-Rhin, France. The family included sons Jacob, George, Charles, William, and Fred along with daughters Louise and Magdalena (nicknamed Lany). By 1880 their father, George, had died. Most of the siblings were still living at home at the time, including Louise who now had the last name of Shaw and was living in Lyons with a daughter named Magdalena (nicknamed Lena). The boys were all working to support the family. The exact date is unclear, but it was sometime in the late 1800s when the family relocated to Batavia.

According to the 1900 Federal census Fred lived with his mother on Ross Street, and she reported giving birth to ten children seven of whom were still alive at that time. Their mother died in 1906 and by that time Charles had moved into the Ross

Street house. The 1910 census lists Fred, Charles and his wife Carrie living on Ross Street. Their brother William and his family had moved into the house next door.

Before coming to Seven Springs, Fred worked at the Dellinger Theater in Batavia as the stage manager. He also worked as a wallpaper hanger and painter for a man named Frank Cross. As an interesting side note, when the repairs were done on the 'Yellow Cottage" in 1930 one of the walls was signed by Fred, Frank and a third man named Scott Washburn. The signatures were discovered during recent (2020) renovations of the cottage.

The New York State census records show that Fred had moved to Seven Springs by 1925. However, according to his obituary he built his three room Seven Springs cabin in 1918. Over the years many articles mentioned Fred and his home, and they painted a lovely picture of his quiet cabin in the woods. He designed and built his cottage after being given permission to build on the spot of his choice. He called the cottage "Millers Rest". Water came from a spring beneath the cottage, and he did most of his cooking on a wood stove. Fred's snug home contained a Victrola that he used to enjoy his music - opera and classical being his favorite. He also enjoyed spending time reading and canning a wide variety of foods for the winter months. He modernized the cabin after a time and added a radio to listen to the news. For many years, his cabin had the only telephone on the property.

Fred lived a very simple life and credited that fact for his longevity. He also believed that his daily habit of drinking a small glass of lemon juice everyday helped. He enjoyed putting both small and large meals for members of the Club and very often served a meal for the Club's annual meeting and for other events, sometimes serving upwards of 85 people. Yet, the thing that Fred was most well-known for was his ability to predict the weather.

Many local publications considered Fred to be a weather prophet. He was, in fact, known throughout the state and beyond for his accuracy. His obituary published in the *Buffalo Courier-Express* stated "His predictions were carried on national press wires and often proved accurate." Fred was often contacted by local newspapers to give his prediction on a coming winter. One such prediction appeared in a Herkimer, N.Y. newspaper in 1954. Mr. Miller said the following: "I watch the caterpillars at this time of year. Nature has provided only a thin fur cover for the caterpillars this fall. This fact and the scarcity of butternuts and walnuts indicate it will be a mild winter." On another occasion the *Batavia Daily News* reached out by phone to him to discuss particularly changeable weather conditions one spring. Fred was quoted as saying "Everything's mixed up and even the government weathermen are having their troubles". He mentioned that someone from the Farm Bureau had visited him that week to discuss the weather conditions. Fred was predicting a much anticipated warm up after a difficult winter. He pointed to the position and brightness of the moon as well as to the sounds made by his dining room table. He said the table would always creak whenever weather changes were about to occur.

In 1929, Fred became the Club's Superintendent, following the death of Edward Russell. He was 66 years old at the time and his salary was $400 per year. He spent the next several decades devoting his considerable energy and talents to the betterment of Seven Springs. At the time of his retirement from service his annual salary had increased to $600.

Fred continued to live in Seven Spring into his nineties. He moved to the Genesee County Home a few months before his death. In 1960, at the age of 96, Fred Miller died at the County Home. According to his obituary, he continued to make the two mile walk into Batavia for food and supplies weekly until he was almost 90. He also chopped his own firewood and continued to hold the position of Club superintendent until the year before he moved to the County Home. Fred is buried at Grandview Cemetery in Batavia next to his sister Louise Shaw

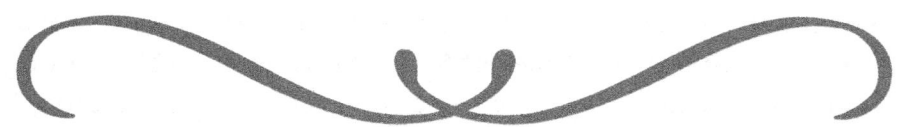

CHAPTER 7
The Russell Family

Edward Russell was born in 1855 to John and Mary O'Brien Russell. Both of his parents were born in Ireland, most likely in County Tipperary. They emigrated to the U.S. and lived in Wyoming County before settling with their family in Batavia. Their son Edward married Katherine Kenney in about 1876. The couple lived on West Main Street where they raised six children: Frank, William, Edward, Mary, Anna, and Raymond. Edward spent several years working as a teacher. He later worked as a grocer and served as an Alderman for the City of Batavia. Following his retirement, Edward spent the last 17 years of his life dedicated to building Seven Springs from a swampy pasture to a wooded property with a man-made lake. He himself planted many of the thousands of trees that were cultivated to develop the woods. Edward died at his West Main Street home on April 6, 1929, at the age of 75.

The establishment of the Seven Springs Country Club was made possible by Edward and his son William "Billy" Russell, beginning with the purchase of the Seven Springs property by Billy. Edward had always admired the land, and after Billy purchased it, Edward set to work on contacting local businessmen and organizing the formation of the Club. He served as President of Seven Springs from 1911 until his death in 1929. Edward was officially appointed Caretaker of Seven Springs in 1921, although he had functioned in that role since the beginning of the Club, He was also designated as the Special Deputy Sheriff as part of his role.

The Russell children were a talented bunch; several of them were known for their interest in the theatre and performing arts. The ones who were not performers were involved in theatre support and design as well as the arts. In 1947 William was quoted as saying "I can't remember when we all became interested in show business, and it almost seems as if it were something born in us. Neither one of our parents was interested in it. But it's been very interesting, and we've had some good times with it all". The following paragraphs further highlight the lives of members of the Russell family.

Frank "Pop": Frank married Agnes Rimmer and they had a daughter named Mary. He made his living as a realtor but was most well-known as a member of the Batavia Players. Frank performed in many productions as well as helped to build sets. His daughter Mary followed in his footsteps as she was also actively involved in the theatre group. Mary became a teacher in Batavia and Attica, in 1952 she died at the age of 42. Frank lived to the age of 88, having passed away in 1966.

William "Billy": Seven Springs owes a tremendous amount to the Russell family. It is not an exaggeration to say that without Billy Russell it may not exist at all. Billy was a renowned magician, and the following information appeared in his obituary: "Mr. Russell had worked with the nations and world's leading magicians. Mr. Russell launched his career in 1895, traveling throughout the United States with his "Russell's Magic Circus". He built equipment for Harry Houdini and was a friend of Howard Thurston and Blackstone." Billy developed Houdini's famous Milk Can Escape and his Paper Bag Escape. After his traveling circus days ended, he settled back in Batavia. He married Renetta Lachnicht in 1910, and they had no children. Billy's home was on West Main Street, however he spent considerable time in Seven Springs and served as its President. His cottage was known as the "Red Raven", where he hosted many parties for his fellow magicians. He remained active in the community and was the President of the local chapter of the International Brotherhood of Magicians. He lived in Batavia until his death in 1966 at the age of 86.

Edward "Ned": Ned worked as a sound man in theaters in the early 1900's. He travelled the country providing sound to early movies. As "talkies" became the standard in the movie industry, his skills as a sound man were no longer needed. Ned moved back to the area, settling in Buffalo, and marrying Grace Elizabeth Feltes in 1912. He was also well-known around the area as a ventriloquist but made his living as an interior decorator. Ned and Grace had one daughter, Ruth. He died in Buffalo in January 1971 at the age of 87.

Mary "Bess": Bess was the fourth child of Edward and Katherine and their first daughter. Mary married Edward McMannis, and the couple had no children. After her husband Edward's death at Seven Springs, Bess took over his real estate business. She became a realtor and was active in the Batavia community until her death at the age of 89 in 1976.

Anna: Anna married Rue Kelsey in 1914, and they had a daughter named Madeline. Anna was widowed in 1925 and never remarried. After the death of her husband Anna and her daughter lived in the same house as her mother and sister. She eventually moved in with her daughter's family in Sheldon, N.Y. Anna was active and involved in many organizations in Batavia. Much like her siblings, Anna lived a long life. She died at the age of 85 in 1975.

Raymond: On the 1920 census Raymond's occupation was listed as a newspaper cartoonist living in Batavia. In the 1920's he married wife Margaret. They lived for a time in Minnesota, and they had three sons. They eventually made their way further west, moving to California, where he worked as an artist at MGM Studios. Raymond was the only one of his siblings who did not live into his eighties. He was 50 at the time of his death in 1946.

SECTION IV

Building it Up

CHAPTER 8
Conservation

Seven Springs Country Club was formed with the intention of preserving and improving the land. At the time of incorporation in 1911 it comprised 55 acres of land in the Bigelow Creek watershed. It was said that there were seven known and named springs. When purchased, the land was filled with underbrush and was a mix of swampy and bare land. Some parts were home to a sheep pasture, with minimal vegetation and a few small trees. The beautiful, wooded land and lake that is seen today is the direct result of the early founders and their vision for Seven Springs.

A variety of species of trees have been planted through the years, and that work continues to this day. In the early days it was unclear if trees would grow well on the land. Seven Springs members worked with New York State forestry experts, and it was decided to begin planting Scotch pine along with White and Red Pine trees. This was soon followed by plantings of Norway Spruce from Saranac, New York, and White Cedar.

One of the more unusual headlines related to Seven Springs appeared in an article on the front page of *The Buffalo News* in

1929. The headline read, "Reforestation of Batavia Tract Largely the Work of Hoboes". The article shared the following about the project: "Itinerant workers were picked up by sponsors of the project and employed to set out the thousands of trees furnished by the state. That was in 1912." An earlier passage in the article mentions that Western New York was experiencing an industrial depression. Presumably the founders of the Club hired those out-of-work to plant the trees.

In the 1920's there was a renewed interest in conservation throughout the state of New York. People from across the state were interested in planting and reforestation. Western New York was seen as a good example of successful reforestation thanks in no small part to the actions of Seven Springs. A 1921 *Batavia Daily News* article detailed the difficulties in growing a forest from nearly bare land. The article states that 100 English Walnut trees had recently been planted to add to the existing species planted in the years before. It had been the intention of the Club to plant new trees every year beginning in 1912. Almost all the plantings did not survive the first year. In 1913 more trees were planted and they thrived due in large measure to the care they received from Edward Russell. He protected the young trees from deep snows by clearing the snow from them. It was said in the article that trees that were six inches high when planted in 1913 had grown to fifteen feet by 1921. The article goes on to describe the success of the forestry efforts as follows: "Foresters from all parts of the country come to the Seven Springs every year to inspect the work and to take pictures which are used for lecture courses."

A 1922 article in the *Leroy Gazette* states that Seven Springs had planted approximately 30,000 trees. This was second only to County Home in Bethany. In June of 1929 a tour was organized to showcase some of the good work done in our area. The two-day tour of Western New York began at Seven Springs. The group consisted of 250 people representing 20 different counties touring the area before ending at Letchworth State Park.

In 1925 a grove of 700 Maple trees was planted at the southeast corner of the property. In 2002 with the help of several members and many hours of labor, the trees were tapped, and the syrup was boiled down in a large caldron. The resulting maple syrup was delicious.

By 1929 the Club had planted a reported 40,00 trees including: Red, White and Scotch Pine, Spruce, Balsam, Cedar, Hemlock, Larch, Maple, English Walnut, among others.

In the 2000's two forestry projects were undertaken to harvest hardwoods to sell. The profits have helped to defray operating and maintenance costs in Seven Springs. Following the path of the early founders to this day new trees are being planted. The current focus is the planting of mixed hardwoods to replace any harvested trees. Several children of current members have helped with the planting of these trees. The hope is to introduce the next generation to the beauty of the surrounding place and the importance of proper forestry practices.

CHAPTER 9
The Road

When Seven Springs was first formed, members entered from Gardner's Pond Road at what is now the back gate (recently renamed as Grist Mill Road). In 1914 a road was surveyed and built, and it was described in *The Batavia Daily News* as follows: "leading from the dam at the lower end of the lake up over the hill and around the grove to meet the road that comes into the grounds from the south"

A fence around the property was installed in 1917. It was decided in 1923 that gates should be constructed, with steel-frame gates placed at both entrances. The gates were to be always locked with a key given to each member. The back entrance still has parts of the original gates. At that time the front gates were located where the current stone and brick sign stands. Documentation from 1932 shows that the Directors wanted to move the front gates to the back entrance and design a new front gate; however, no further documentation was found to confirm if they were moved. Decades later, new gates were constructed at the front entrance in 1960 by member Howard Seeley. The stone was brought from Lake Ontario. It took four trips to bring all the stone and Mr. Seeley submitted a bill for $55.55 for his costs. The back entrance still has parts of the original steel gates.

Next in 1932, the front entrance to Seven Springs was redesigned. Bricks were added between the original gate posts, creating the long decorative sign that exists today. The new entrance was placed directly across from John O'Brien's house. It was redesigned for safer traffic flow in and out of the property. However, it wasn't until the late 1970's or early 1980's when the road was paved for the first time. By that time most of the cottages were occupied year-round and there was increased traffic through the Springs. Paving the road cut down on dust and dirt as well as made the road safer. Later in the early 2000's the road was repaired and repaved. Every year members spend time repairing and patching to keep the road in good shape.

CHAPTER 10
The Dam

The lake is a focal point of Seven Springs. With its cold, clear water, it is one of the most beautiful and unique features of this place. It is hard to imagine Seven Springs without the lake, but when the club was first formed it did not exist. There were seven known springs in the early 1900s which is how it got its name. An August 1912 article in a Batavia newspaper stated that planning and construction was underway for a dam. The area that became the lake was a swampy field with brush and low growth. Once the field was cleared of much of the vegetation, construction was started.

The dam was designed by member Andrew Clough. It was made of concrete and was built nine feet high and just over 100 feet long with a road over the top.

An article in the *Daily News* in April of 1913 describes the construction as follows "President Russell of the club, with a few assistants closed the opening in the dam by dropping six-inch slabs of reinforced concrete into slots prepared for them and the water raised so rapidly that it was running over the six-and-a-half-foot dam in less than 48 hours." The resulting lake is roughly five acres in size and holds an estimated seven million gallons of water. The water spills over the dam and feeds the pond at Chapin Mill and then travels on into Bigelow Creek which flows to Horseshoe Lake and Godfrey's Pond.

In those early years the lake was formed for the purpose of fishing and was stocked with brown trout. The Club worked with conservation officials in deciding what type of fish would be best in the cold water. Brown trout would spawn in nearby pools before making their way into the lake. In the past members were asked to log their catch to keep track of the numbers. To ensure a good catch, for many years electric lights were strung low over the water. They would be switched on to attract insects and, in turn, the fish would jump and eat them. It wasn't exactly sporting, but it made for easy fishing.

Over the years the lake has been restocked over the years and one of the spawning pools has been re-dug. The deepest point is near the dam and is approximately 8 feet deep. There is an abundance of other wildlife including turtles, frogs, geese, ducks, blue herons and most recently egrets. Members often enjoy spending time at the dock or swimming in the cold water. The lake is also bordered by a trail that is a beautiful and peaceful walk.

CHAPTER 11
The Edward Russell Bridge

The Russell Memorial Bridge was built to honor Seven Springs first President and caretaker, Edward Russell. Mr. Russell was a driving force in the formation and growth of the Club. It was shortly after his death in 1929 when plans were made for the construction of the bridge.

The cornerstone was laid for the new bridge on October 16, 1929, and a ceremony was held. As a historical note, the event occurred just days before the infamous stock market crash that led to the Great Depression.

At the time, when the cornerstone was laid, members gathered items and put them into a box. A newspaper article described the event as follows: "Deposited in a glass box, were a copy of the constitution and by-laws, a complete list of the members, a short history of the club, a list of the officers and directors, a copy of The News of May 24th and a copy of the Batavia Times, also a brief tribute to Edward Russell, in whose memory the bridge is erected". A few coins were also added. Remarks were made by President Clough, Mayor Hartley, CM Gillett, and Stephen Brown. Edward's son, Frank Russell read his father's favorite poem titled "The Bridge Builder". Following this ceremony, the new superintendent, Fred Miller hosted attendees for a dinner at his cottage.

The bridge is located just below the caretaker's cottage (the Yellow Cottage) and spans a stream. At the time it was built it was said to lead to the Bergman Spring. President Clough designed the bridge, and it is made from steel, concrete, and cobblestone. Supt Miller was put in charge of completing the construction. Made from steel, concrete, and cobblestone, the construction was completed, and the bridge was formally dedicated in May 1930. According to the *Daily News*, a short address was given by President Clough and Albert Squires and the ribbon was cut by Miss Edna Dibble. 45 people attended the event and dinner was served. The article also mentions that work had begun on a gravel path around the lake.

Today, the bridge still stands and is used on a regular basis for members to walk the very path that was started in 1930. The original plaque on the bridge has been lost and despite an extensive search it was unable to be found. In 2020, member Wayne Younge commissioned a new plaque to be built to replace the original. Plans are also underway to locate the missing cornerstone and glass box.

THE BRIDGE BUILDER
By Will Allen Dromgoole

An old man going a lone highway
Came at the evening, cold and gray,
To a chasm vast and deep and wide,
Through which was flowing a sullen tide.

The old man crossed in the twilight dim;
The sullen stream had no fear for him;'
But he turned, when safe on the other side,
And built a bridge to span the tide.

"Old man," said a fellow pilgrim, near,
"You are wasting strength with building here;
Your journey will end with the ending day;
You never again will pass this way;
You've crossed the chasm, deep and wide-
Why build you this bridge at the evening tide?"

The builder lifted his old gray head:
"Good friend, in the path I have come," he said,
"There followeth after me today,
A youth, whose feet must pass this way.

This chasm, that has been naught to me,
To that fair-haired youth may a pitfall be.
He, too, must cross in the twilight dim;
Good friend, I am building this bridge for him."

SECTION V

Notable Events

CHAPTER 12
Fires

There are few things more frightening in the woods than a fire. Throughout the history of the Club there have been several fires, some more serious than others. The first documented fire in Seven Springs occurred in 1912. A fire was discovered by members who had come to the Springs by chance. The men who were present used water from the stream to put the fire out and their quick action prevented serious damage. The fire was said to have started at the winter camp near the site of the proposed lake. This was most likely near the clubhouse end of the lake. It was not known if the fire resulted from carelessness or something more nefarious. A reward was offered for any information about the cause of the fire, but no further information was found.

One of the most dangerous threats to the woods was the Erie Railroad, which lies at the southern side of the property. The first fire related to the railroad happened in 1925 caused damage to the land and young trees. According to Club records a settlement was reached and the Erie Railroad paid $175 in damages

A far more serious fire occurred in May of 1931. The Board meeting notes from that time state the following: *May 6 we had* *a serious fire caused by sparks from the Erie train starting a fire on the Erie right-of-way and burning in onto our property causing the property damage as follows: 109 trees at $1.25, 21 trees at $12, 23 trees at $75 total= $2161.25. To say nothing of the personal injury of burns and smoke to Supt. Miller, Howard Bell, our neighbor across the Erie (Leon Kinney), and others. Only the prompt assistance of those mentioned and the Fire Chief with fireman and chemicals from Batavia, Parker's hired man Fred Ives, school children, members McMannis, Upson and others saved a great loss."* After all was said and done the railroad only ended up paying $220 restitution to the Club.

Seven Springs was fortunate to have a quick response from caretaker Fred Miller along with several members and neighbors. The most surprising volunteer firefighters of the day were the students from nearby School Number 7. It is hard to imagine school children being called into service to help put out a fire today. Happily, none of the children were injured in the incident but the same could not be said for Superintendent Miller. First on the scene, Supt. Miller was overcome by smoke and was unconscious for a short time. According to the newspaper article, Dr. Gardiner was nearby and able to provide aid. The Fire Department was called and arrived to finish fighting the fire. The proximity and quick actions of the members and neighbors prevented serious injury and more severe damage to the woods.

A few years later, in 1934 a fire started in a pile of leaves in the yard of Donald McKenzie's cottage (current day Rapones). The fire spread quickly but was soon under control with little damage thanks to Mr. McKenzie, Supt. Miller, and others. The only casualty was a wooden railway which had been built by Mr. McKenzie's grandsons some years earlier. The rail had been named the "Toonerville Trolley" and was complete with a switch and a small station. Sadly, the little railway was a complete loss.

The very next year, in 1935 another serious fire destroyed a cottage. A fire was discovered at Thomas Canty's cottage around 11pm (current location of Dan Cavalieri's cottage). Members Larry Gubb and Myron St. John noticed the fire from their nearby cottages. The Fire Department and State Police were quickly summoned, and the neighbors sprang into action. A bucket brigade was formed but the fire was unable to be contained and the cottage was a total loss. Luckily no one was injured, and Mr. Canty rebuilt the cottage.

Decades later, in the early 1980's there was a minor fire also along the rail line Two sets of neighbors decided to play it safe, as they headed to the float in the middle of the lake - with some beverages. Luckily there was no danger from the fire and a good time was had by all.

Seven Springs' most recent (and hopefully last) brush with fire came in 2012. There was a slight miscommunication about a brush fire that resulted in both a fire and police response. The incident was chalked up to a "ceremony" and certainly made a good story for the members involved.

CHAPTER 13
Edward F. McMannis

Edward McMannis became a member of Seven Springs in 1923. As the son-in-law of Edward Russell, he would have been familiar with the club. Edward was born in Belfast Ireland on August 15, 1882, to parents John and Catherine Maguire McMannis. He came to the United States by himself at the age of 18.

Edward married Mary Russell on August 10, 1910, at St. Joseph's Church in Batavia. At the time of their marriage, Edward was living in Poughkeepsie, N.Y. The couple lived for a time in Olean before eventually settling in Batavia. Mr. McMannis made his living selling insurance and real estate. Edward was given permission to build a cottage in the Springs in 1923.

Edward and Mary had no children and were active members of the Batavia community. Although Edward joined the Russell family through marriage, he became the family historian according to a *Buffalo News* notice for a Russell family reunion. Sadly, it was Edward's tragic death that became a part of Seven Springs history. The incident was newsworthy and was reported in both Batavia and Rochester.

The following article appeared in the *Batavia Daily News*,

and the story speaks for itself. The headline read; "Seven Springs Cottager Died in the Water". The article goes on to tell the sad story as follows:

"Edward F. McMannis, fifty, proprietor of the McMannis real estate and insurance agency, drowned in the Seven Springs Country Club Pond late this morning, falling into the water as he attempted to fill a tea kettle with water for the radiator of his automobile. His watch had stopped at 11:26 am indicating that that was the time of the accident. Mr. McMannis had gone to the springs this morning to remove screens and storm windows in his summer cottage, taking his brother-in-law, Frank F. Russell with him. It was shortly before 11am when Mr. McMannis and Mr. Russell started from the latter's house to go to the resort. The car had overheated on the trip from Batavia. All except one or two of the screens had been removed when Mr. McMannis left Mr. Russell to complete the job and started for the pond to get water for his car. He returned in a few minutes and got a broom to break the ice on the pond and fill the teakettle he had taken with him. "It was about twenty minutes later when I wondered why he hadn't returned and I went down to the bridge (over the outlet of the pond) to look for him, "said Mr. Russell. "*The car stood on the bridge and the broom lay on the ice and I could see footprints around the hole he had broken up against the abutment, I realized at once that he must have gone into the water and when I knelt down and looked into the hole, I saw the edge of his overcoat. I pulled him out on the ice, and he came out feet first. The ice was cracking all around me, but I managed to get him up out of the water. I tried to get him up on the bridge but couldn't lift him."* (According to the family Mr. McMannis was a large man). At that point Mr. Russell recounted trying to get help. He first went to Supt. Miller's cottage as he had a telephone. He found the cottage empty and was unable to get inside to use the phone. He then went all the way to Mr. Fred Parker's home on East Main Street. The city fire department and the State Police were summoned by 12:05pm, Troopers used a pulmotor and attempted to revive Edward for approximately forty-five minutes without success and the coroner was called to the scene. He was survived by his wife Mary and his brother, John who lived in Belfast, Ireland.

Mary never remarried and her family said that after his death, she did not go back to Seven Springs. She went on to live for many more years and was involved in many organizations in Batavia. She died in 1976 at the age of 89 and is buried next to her husband in St. Joseph Cemetery in Batavia.

CHAPTER 14
Parties

Since its inception, Seven Springs has hosted many types of parties and events. From small picnic gatherings to large weddings and every kind of event in between have been held on the property. Below are some of the more notable events that have happened over the years.

1911- The first documented party at Seven Springs was reported by the Batavia *Daily News* in September. The members gathered for a clambake. Eight-five members and their guests enjoyed steamed clams and other treats.

1913- An afternoon of games and contests was held in late August. The event was put on by the Genesee County Fish and Game Protection Association. It was billed as a field day and there were many competitive games including shooting and casting games. Various prizes were awarded throughout the day and dinner was served.

1915- Twenty students, who were part of an Italian class, enjoyed a spring picnic in Seven Springs. According to the *Batavia Daily News* "The afternoon was devoted to boating, athletic contests and gathering wildflowers and wandering about the little tract of rustic loveliness."

1919- The Women's Civic League in Batavia held a summer lunch at Seven Springs. The article announcing the event was quite detailed. The *Batavia Daily News* reported that every woman in Genesee County was eligible to attend the picnic. The instructions for people to get to the Springs were especially interesting, as there was a Chairman of Transportation who was responsible for coordinating transport. Arriving by automobile was one option, and the Chairman kept a list to arrange rides for those wishing to attend. Attendees were also given the option to take the electric streetcar and advised that the entrance was "a mere 1.4-1.5 miles from the end of the streetcar". Directions were as follows: "It is reached by the East Main Street Road and turning north on the road a short distance west of the Lehigh Valley crossing". Women were asked to bring a lunch and table setting, with coffee to be provided by the Women's League. The article mentioned a guest speaker had been arranged for the outing and ended by stating the outing would be an opportunity for discussion "regarding the many important things that the woman of Genesee County can accomplish".

1923- Board meeting notes discussed forming a committee to make plans for a mortgage burning and celebratory party for Seven Springs members. The notes from the meeting further describe the purpose of the event as follows; "to act in arranging an outing for all members, a feed and general jollification with the burning of the mortgage as the climax"

1926 - Many parties were hosted by William Russell for fellow magicians. The following notification appeared in a magician's magazine called *The Billboard* on July 31, 1926"

"William A Russell, the Batavia NY magician, entertained a number of his friends, members of the Magicians' Club of Buffalo, July 18 at his Seven Springs cottage, the Red Raven. There were 20 present, including some of the magicians wives and children. Following the dinner, the magicians put on a short entertainment at the Seven Springs Clubhouse to which the members of Seven Springs Country Club and guests were invited. The guests were given a preview of some of the feats of magic which had been worked out since last season. The impromptu entertainment was witnessed by a full house and the audience included many children."

The article goes on to mention a performance given by Adam Ross who was a magician and well-known ventriloquist. The Red Raven was sold to Adam Ross in 1963 after which it was knocked down and rebuilt.

1927- The International Brotherhood of Magicians (IBM) held their annual party in Seven Springs at the Clubhouse. William Russell was elected as President of Ring Four which was the Western New York chapter of the IBM. The Clubhouse was reportedly decorated with posters and pictures of magicians. A vaudeville act was performed, and Mr. Russell gave a talk to those in attendance.

1929 - William Russell hosted The International Brotherhood of Magicians again at the Red Raven. The group included magicians of Ring Four yet again.

1929 - Halloween parties have been popular in recent years, but they are not new to Seven Springs. Frank Russell's daughter, Miss Mary Russell, held one such party in October of 1929. The *Batavia Daily News* described the party by saying that Miss Russell "delightfully entertained forty friends at a Halloween party at the Seven Springs Country Club".

1933 - The week of August 17, 1933, was a busy one at Seven Springs. In the *Batavia Times* Society News there was mention of four different parties held on the grounds. St. Joseph's Church held a dinner on Thursday of that week. Guests were served a steak fry. On Saturday, the Clough and Bridge families held a picnic in honor of a newlywed couple, Mr. and Mrs. Fred Wilcox. The couple was given an electric clock as a gift. The following Monday Mrs. Bridge hosted the Garden and Bird Club at a picnic at her cottage. Thirty members of her club were present. Finally, on the next Thursday Mrs. Melvin Tyler held a meeting of the Ideal Home Bureau at her cottage, with supper served.

1934- A rather curious picnic was held this year. It was so interesting that it was discussed at the annual meeting of the Club in May. The meeting minutes documented the Board's discussion of an event termed "promiscuous picnicking" that had occurred. Consequently, a resolution was passed that stated "A member must be present at and responsible for all gatherings. You must not loan your keys". No further documentation was found to give details of the offending event.

1937- One of the most interesting groups that held gatherings at Seven Springs was the Klondikers. They were a group of men who had been a part of the Alaska gold rush right before the turn of the century. The group met at the Clubhouse yearly to reminisce about the days of the gold rush. In March of 1937 when one such reunion was held, the group included about 50 members. A few of the members who were present inspected the property and even panned for gold in the stream. Unfortunately, no gold was found. The *Batavia Times* article stated: "Most of the "sourdoughs" walked around without topcoats or overcoats, loudly proclaiming their disgust for the "sissy" winter weather.". The Klondikers continued to meet at Seven Springs into the 1940s.

In the 1950's there were several mentions of meetings held by the Batavia Lions Club. The Batavia Daily News published a notice in 1957 that mentioned how members of the Lions Club helped to make repairs to the Clubhouse.

1959- The Batavia Society of Artists held an all-day sketch party. Participants were invited to spend the day sketching the surroundings followed by a dinner. Prizes were awarded at the end of the event.

Throughout the next few decades there were numerous mentions of parties held at Seven Springs. Some of the organizations that were mentioned were: the Byron Garden Club, Byron Presbyterian Church, Genesee County Bar Association, Lions Club, Older Boys Club, Allied Youth Post, and the Redfield Parkway Association. Also, the following church groups that held events at Seven Springs: Batavia First United Methodist, Byron Presbyterian Church, the Knights of Columbus, First Baptist Church.

In addition to the above events, Seven Springs has played host to many weddings over the years. For example, in the 1980's the William's family had a wedding, with guests shuttled to and from the reception. In the 1990's and early 2000's beautiful and unique weddings were held by the McGees, the Posts and the Carvers.

    Over the years the beautiful setting of the Springs has played host to many celebrations and events. Our hope is that this tradition will continue for decades to come.

SECTION VI

Photos

A. Clough, Edward Russell, and unknown 1920s

Dedication of Edward Russel Bridge 1930

The dock through the years...

SEVEN SPRINGS COUNTRY CLUB

Katy Greene 1990s

The original paddle boat 1980s

The Post family 1980s

Gabe Post, 1984

Jennifer Carver supervising the addition to her house.

Greg Post 1980s

Work at the Yellow Cottage 1980s

Ed Ferris, Eddie Ferris, Shane Carver 1983

Greg Post and Shane Carver 1980s

Outdoor fireplace 1980s

The Original Fairy House 1980s

SEVEN SPRINGS COUNTRY CLUB

Shane Carver 1983

1993- front: Mary Carver, Rita Brenkus, Cody Balling
back: Cheryl Manz, Melissa Post, Jennifer Carver

2002 Maple Syrup Jason and James Reardon, Joan Post, Joe Manz

2002 Clambake: Jason and James Reardon, Joe Manz, Daryl Kohorst, Greg Post

The Little Library and Militia Bell 2021. Wayne Younge and Joe Nicosia

2021 Marcy Crandall and Tom Kowal

2021 Tad Gerace, Ryan Ross, Cindy Lewis, Joan Post.

SECTION VII

The Neighbors

CHAPTER 15
The Mason Family

F.E (Frank). Mason began his career as an art gun engraver, working for the Baker Gun Company in Batavia. In 1907 he started his own business making foil embossed labels. The labels featured intricate designs created by using hand drawn die cuts. The unique designs were made using a combination of foil, paper and gum backing. The business was in operation until 1972, when less expensive mass-produced labels replaced the unique hand-made designs.

    F.E. and his wife, Elizabeth had three children, Roy, Nina Mason Booth and Max Sr. Roy was perhaps the most well-known but all three of the children were talented artists in their own right. Roy and Max both worked at the family business. Nina and Roy had a commercial art studio in Philadelphia in the early 1900's. When Nina married Herbert Booth, they made their home in Batavia. Roy and his wife eventually moved west to California where he pursued his art career. Max Sr. stayed in their home at Woodchuck Hollow, as detailed below. Eventually Max Mason Jr.

and his brother-in-law, John Bertrand took over the running of the family business. Max Jr. and his wife Jane built a home behind his parents' house. They raised their children, Suzy and Marc and lived in their home for several decades. They were also long-time members of Seven Springs. Max died in 2016 and Jane in 2017. In addition to being early members of Seven Springs, the Mason family also helped found the Stafford Country Club. Max Sr. and Roy were raised in a home on East Main St. in Batavia, moving to Seven Springs Road as adults.

It was 1937 when Max and Roy Mason purchased the tract of land west of Larry Gubb and Gardner's Pond and Seven Springs in 1937. The thirty-three-acre tract of land was purchased from James Bratt. The area was known as "Woodchuck Hollow". The brothers built 2 homes about 100 yards apart, and even though they were close, the homes were very different. The plans for the homes were detailed in the *Batavia Daily News* which described Roy Mason's plans as follows: "The residence will be constructed of field stone and timber with a living room about 30 by 17 feet in size. There will be an art gallery to house Mr. Mason's valuable collection of paintings by famous artists. A loom room will be provided for Mrs. Mason, who is interested in the weaving of tapestries." The article went on to say that servant's quarters would be included in the plans. Max Mason's home was described as a colonial design. It was said that before the trees in the woods matured, it was possible to see Prole Road from the Mason property.

Roy's home served as inspiration for his work and hosted many artists over the years. One famous guest was the painter Andrew Wyeth who visited along with his parents in 1939. Other prominent American artists who visited the Mason home include Rockwell Kent, Tore Asplund, the Wittakers, Chauncy Ryder. and Norman Kent.

1921 Max Mason Jr., Constance Mason, and Unknown

CHAPTER 16
The Chapin Mill Retreat Center

The Chapin Mill Retreat Center sits on 135 acres of land bordering Seven Springs Country Club. It is a serene and beautiful setting that is well suited as the setting of a meditation retreat center.
An early owner of the land was named Seymour Ensign and the area was called Ensign's Hollow or Ensign's Pond. The pond was formed, and the grist mill built in 1809 followed by the Mill House in 1811. The grist mill was reportedly the first in all of Genesee County and was in operation for 80 years. The next owner was a Mr. Gardiner who built the barn and other outbuildings. The pond then became known as "Gardner's Pond". A Reverend Ezra Hammond also lived for a time in the Mill House. He started a mill to plane wood and the Seven Springs Clubhouse was made from wood that came from Hammond's mill.

Gardiner's Pond was next purchased by Larry Gubb in 1934. Mr. Gubb, a native of the area, was an executive of the Philco Company and bought the property for use as a summer home. During the time he lived there horse stables and a riding camp were established.

In 1948 Ralph Chapin purchased the Gubb property, and he lived there until his death in 2000. His family honored the land and planted many trees and gardens to enhance its beauty. Ralph was also a founding member of the Rochester Zen Center. In 1996 he donated his property to fulfill the Center's dream of building a meditation retreat center. The original structures- the Mill House, farmhouse, and barn- all still stand. The newer structures are the retreat center (completed in 2010) and caretaker's home, known as Klava House (completed in 2020 and named after the former Chain property caretaker, Laimons Klava). Today the buildings and surrounding land are used by the Zen Center as well as other groups for meditation retreats.

SECTION VIII

The Cottages

CHAPTER 17
Cottage History

Research the history of the cottages as Seven Springs Country Club was a complex process. The following information was gathered from the records of the Club and Genesee County, as well as newspaper articles and oral histories A variety of techniques had to be used to find the most complete and accurate information available. Any errors or omissions are unintentional.

Genesee County identifies build dates for most of the existing cottages. However, because the cottages do not have traditional deeds, it is unclear how the County obtained this information. When the cottages were first built the taxes were split among members. As more cottages were added, they were eventually individually assessed and taxed. It is likely that the build dates are approximate and, in some cases, simply incorrect. It is also likely that the Club's records may reflect an earlier structure that was removed and rebuilt, which in turn could affect the accuracy of the County's information. In some cases, the records refer to "moveable bungalows" or tents being placed. After the original structures were erected cottages that were added later, were noted as being located north or east, etc. of a particular cottage. If the location of the first cottage was unknown or no longer there, it was difficult to figure out the location of the structures that followed.

A blueprint made in 1924 identified possible building sites for individual camps. This map marked many small sites stretching from the dam to the Erie RR line (near the present-day Pink Candle). These spots were numbered from one to sixty-six and followed the line of the original road through Seven Springs. However, this original map looks different from present day Seven Springs and is somewhat difficult to reconcile. It does include the location of many existing structures but does not correspond to the current numbering system. This map was revised in 1933, when members decided the proposed sites were too close together. The sites were then changed to allow for more space between structures.

Beginning in 1945 the Club began keeping a list of cottages and owners for tax purposes. In 1976 a numbering system was devised. Cottage one was the clubhouse, cottage two (present day Eddie and Teresa Ferris' home), cottage 3 (present day Wayne Younge's home), etc. Numbers continued in order on the lakeside moving across to the other side ending with cottage 20, the present-day Pink Candle. Cottages twenty-one and twenty-two are located on the main Seven Springs Road. Some cottages still have a plaque with these numbers on them.

At some point, all the cottages were given Seven Springs Road addresses by the Postal Service. Cottages within the Springs were given addresses that began with number five, while homes on Seven Springs Road began with number eight. Somehow the home owned by Max and Jane Mason was given the same address as another one of the cottages within the Springs. Max and Jane had a security alarm, and the police would often show up to the wrong house.

The confusion with the addresses also caused problems for emergency services and package deliveries. Consequently, in 2019 Genesee County decided to change the system. Seven Springs Country Club was assigned four separate roads, each with its own name, and a new cottage numbering system was put in place. The

Chapin Mill Retreat Center was also given new road names and structure numbers at the same time. The roads within the Club were named after four men or families who have had profound impacts on the development of Seven Springs:

Russell Road - named after Edward Russell, founder the first caretaker of Seven Springs

Miller Springs Road - named after long-time caretaker Fred Miller.

Hawkins Hollow Road- named after long-time member and President Ernie Hawkins

Canty Lane- named after long-time member and contributor Thomas Canty and his family

CHAPTER 18
The Clubhouse

Miller Springs Road
Known as: Cottage #1 and "The Clubhouse"

Construction on the Clubhouse was started in 1925 after the property's mortgage had been paid off. The location was described as a "clearing in the grove formerly used as a picnic ground".
At the Annual meeting on May 24, 1924, the following information was provided: "The property is now free of debt and in good position to finance a Club House and Shelter which will probably be taken up next year as our neighbor Mr. Hammond is putting in a mill at Gardiner's Pond and suitable timber can be cut out of our woods and cut at this mill with considerable savings made."
By 1925 building plans had been firmed up, at a June 1925 meeting the following was decided: *"It was decided that the fireplace be eliminated for the present, that a basement be made under*

the building proper (20x36x7), that the veranda floor be concrete (10x36), the ceiling posts 10 feet and the Assembly Room 20x26 and the kitchen, 20x10." Lumber and materials were estimated at $725 and labor $300. An additional $400 was estimated for excavation and cement for the basement.

Two years later, in May of 1927, The Club's annual meeting was held for the first time in the new Clubhouse, and they have taken place there each year ever since. Over the years a variety of other kinds of events have also taken place at the Clubhouse. Many organizations have rented the space for picnics and members have used it for birthdays, reunions, and parties. Several weddings have also been held there.

A number of renovations to the Clubhouse have been undertaken over time. In 1981, new tables and chairs were purchased. A year later, in 1982, the fireplace was built and dedicated to President Hawkins. In 1989, the main room of the Clubhouse was renovated with a new ceiling and walls, along with a kitchen remodel. Most recently, in 1995 an addition was made to the structure in order to add two bathrooms, and the windows were replaced.

CHAPTER 19
The Yellow Cottage

Location: Miller Springs Road
Known as: The "Caretakers Cottage", and the "The Yellow Cottage"

The Yellow Cottage has served many purposes over the years. In 1915 there is documentation of a 14' x 20' building constructed as a place to work from. Notes from 1923 further state that as the Club caretaker, Edward Russell was given exclusive use of the "club cottage" at the head of the lake. A few years later, in 1926, the Board passed a motion as follows: "The Russell cottage was ordered to be sealed up and bedroom partition put in with plasterboard or like material." It is unclear if Mr. Russell was still using the cottage regularly at that time.

A year later, in 1930, more work was done on the cottage when it was decided that suitable rest rooms and sanitary toilets should be provided in the "Russell Club Cottage". In the process of a renovation project started in 2020, signatures were uncovered on the wood sheathing that date back to when that work was done. The recent efforts to remodel the Yellow Cottage have been led by Springs resident Wayne Younge. Improvements involve gutting and replacing the interior and adding new water and gas lines. The project has been assisted by students from BOCES building trades, including Springs resident Thomas Reardon. Students helped by shoring up the foundation and getting the cottage ready for electrical updates.

CHAPTER 20
Cottage #2

Location: Miller Springs Road

Fred Miller was given permission to build a "moveable bungalow" at this location in 1921. The original structure was 14x20 feet. In 1948 the cottage was assessed at $650. Mr. Miller made his home in Seven Springs for many years, and there are numerous references to the many dinners he prepared and hosted in his cottage. Upon the death of Edward Russell in 1929, Fred was made the caretaker of Seven Springs.

Records show that by 1959 Fred Miller had moved to the County Home and the cottage was then sold to Mr. Grundler. In 1961 the cottage was purchased by Harold Seekins. He lived there until 1981 when it was purchased by Laverne Pangrazio and Jacqueline Smith. The next owner was Everett Norris who purchased it in 1986. By 1994 the cottage had changed hands again and was owned by Mike Pieri. The Club took ownership of the cottage in 1999 after it had fallen into disrepair, and left was vacant until it was purchased by Ed Ferris in 2009. Ed and his wife Teresa have spent several years working on the cottage, putting on an addition in 2013.

CHAPTER 21
Cottage #3

Location: Russell Road

While Genesee County records show that Cottage #3 was built in 1915, the Club's records don't show a cottage at this location until the late 1960s. Steve Brocker, a Batavia fireman, was listed as the owner on the 1969 tax assessment. It is possible that a cottage was built on this spot in the early 1900s, although it had been an empty lot when the current one was built.

In 1981 the cottage was purchased by Frank Pieri. He put a 10'x20' addition on the year after he purchased the cottage. He then sold the cottage in 1990/91 to Ignatius Radesi who lived there until 1995. The next owner was David Thompson, and he lived there until his death in 2013. The cottage was next purchased by Wayne Younge. In 2014 Wayne built a large deck at the back of the cottage known as the "Crow's Nest"; it has one of the best lake views in the Springs. Many entertaining gatherings have occurred there, and thus the saying, "What happens in the Crow's Nest, stays in the Crow's Nest."

CHAPTER 22
Cottage #4

Location: Russell Road

Like many of the cottages that have been researched, the county build date is difficult to reconcile with the Clubs records. The earliest documented owner of Cottage #4 is A.H. Gover who shows up on the 1954 tax assessment roll. The Govers were the owners until 1971 when it was purchased by Jack and Regina Ahl. The Ahls owned the small cottage for several years before selling it to their daughter and son in law, Joyce and Daryl Kohorst in 1993. The Korhorsts currently rent the cottage to Bill Windahl, and he has lived there for several years.

When the new addresses were being assigned by the county in 2019 it was discovered that this cottage had never had a formal address. After going through all the paperwork, he had from the purchase of the home, Mr. Kohorst could find no address. Because the cottage had mainly been used as a seasonal home, all correspondence and bills had gone to the main address of whoever the owner was. For the first time in history, the little red cottage has finally been given an address

CHAPTER 23
Cottage #5

Location: Russell Road

Ernest Childs was among the first members of Seven Springs, joining in 1912. He was given permission to build a cottage in 1933. Ernest and his wife were the owners until about 1948 when it was sold to Ward Legg. Mr. Legg owned the cottage until 1953 when Gordon Yauchzee purchased it. Mr. Yauchzee informed the Board of his plans to build a cottage on "the lot east of Alfred Govers cottage." It is likely he took down an existing structure and built the current cottage. Mr. Yauchzee owned the cottage for many years.

Between 1976 and 1981 the cottage was sold to Richard Callan. He owned it until 1983 when it was purchased by June and James Simpson. The Simpson's remodeled the cottage the same year they bought it. Mr. Simpson passed away not long after he and his wife moved in. June Simpson continued to live there until her death in 1993 when it was passed to a family member named Maloney. However, the cottage sat empty for a period of time after June's death. During the summer of 1993 there was a series of burglaries in Batavia, and it was later discovered that the thieves were bringing their stolen goods back to the vacant cottage and storing them. A kind neighbor even unknowingly helped the thieves throw away a rug in the dumpster! The police figured it all out. They staked out the cottage until the thieves showed up with more stolen items and arrested them.

A year later, in 1994, the cottage was purchased by Walt and Bob Shell, and then it was sold to Patrick and Peggy Weissend. In turn, Pat sold the cottage to his nephew, Joe Nicosia, in 2009. Joe and his wife Kim Przybysz extensively remodeled the cottage, changing the entire layout. They also added a garage in 2018.

CHAPTER 24
Cottage #6

Location: Russell Road

The county records show the cottage was built in 1952, however like many other cottages it was likely rebuilt at this time. The earliest known owner of cottage #6 is Asher Davis who was the owner in the 1940's. Albert Roda became the owner about 1945/47 and later passed the cottage to his son Everett. The Roda's sold it to Rex Zilliman in late 1959. Zilliman only owned it for a short time before it was sold to Roy McCabe in 1960. McCabe owned it for many years before selling it to Greg Post and his family. Greg did a lot of work remodeling the cottage, putting on a large addition in the early 1980s that added two rooms to the back. The cottage had a lot of character with hand painted art on the walls and a totem pole in the front yard. A wrap-around deck was also built, and a basement was dug.

In 1991 Jim and Kay McGee purchased the cottage from

the Post family. It was Jim's dream house, as he loved the woods and the water. Sadly, just a few months after moving in, Jim passed away unexpectedly. Kay took over the membership and the cottage and lived there until her death in 2014. During the time Kay lived there she renovated the kitchen and had central air installed. The McGee's daughters, Eileen and Mary Ellen are the current cottage owners, with Eileen residing there. Recent renovation projects include rebuilding the deck and the shed.

CHAPTER 25
Cottage #7

Location: Russell Road

Carl Wartusch is the first documented owner of this cottage beginning about 1945-47. The county lists 1920 as the build date. Mr. Wartusch was likely not the first owner, but records are unclear before this time. The next owner was Ernest Riegle and his wife, Evelyn who purchased the cottage in 1949. Mrs. Riegle's parents, Mr. and Mrs. Stroh were already members and cottage owners at the time. The Riegles owned the cottage for several years before selling to William and Amelia Griswold in 1961. Shortly after buying the cottage, Mr. Griswold passed away. Mrs. Griswold, who was known as Faye, was a housekeeper for the Chapin family, whose property borders the Springs (present-day Chapin Mill Retreat Center). She made the cottage her year-round home until 1983 when it was sold to Ed Ferris Sr and his family. When Mr. Ferris brought the cottage; it was in poor shape. Extensive work was done by Mr. Ferris, including a large addition and concrete work in the front of the house. The Ferris family lived here until 1990 when the cottage was sold to Dick and Rita Brenkus. Dick and Rita added to the cottage a large living room and garage below it, resulting in the house's current footprint. The cottage was then sold to Andre Camel in 1995. After his wife's death, Andre converted the basement into his living area. He added a small kitchen area, renovated the bathroom, and built a Murphy bed. In 1999 the cottage was purchased by the current family, the Reardon family.

CHAPTER 26
Cottage #8

Location: Cottage does not exist anymore
Known as: "The Wee Stoll In"

Cottage #8 was located by the Club's back gate and does not exist anymore. Harold Stoll, who became a member in 1949, built the cottage at that time. In 1954 it was still owned by the Stoll's and was called *The Wee Stoll In.* The Stoll's remained owners of the cottage until 1973 when it was purchased by Ron Neth who owned it for 10 years.

Next, in 1983 the cottage was purchased by Donald Smithgall. It eventually fell into disrepair and became a safety hazard. Mr. Smithgall received several letters from the Club asking for him to board up the cottage for safety reasons. In 1988 the cottage was purchased by the Club for $1,500 and decided that it needed to be demolished.

CHAPTER 27
Cottage #9

Location: Cottage no longer part of Seven Springs

Owned and likely built by Larry Gubb, this little cabin in the woods used to be a part of Seven Springs. Mr. Gubb was an executive with the Philco company and owned the land at Gardner's Pond. In 1948 Mr. Gubb sold his rustic cottage to Ralph Chapin, whose property borders the Springs. In 1996 Mr. Chapon donated his land to Rochester Zen Center, including the cottage. Today, the tucked-away little cabin is occasionally used for camping and solo meditation retreats. This is the best example we have of what cottages throughout the Springs many have looked like in early days. To this day the cottage has no electricity or running water.

CHAPTER 28
Cottage #10

Location: Russell Road
Known as: "The Dun Workin' "

This cottage sits atop the hill overlooking the lake. According to the county it was built in 1900, however, this date is likely incorrect as Seven Springs was not formed until after that time. There is documentation that TC Canty was given permission to build a cottage in 1923 on Lot #7. There is also documentation that Mr. Canty took over Mr. Upson's cottage. Mr. Upson was also an early member of Seven Springs and records show that he was cottage owner.

By 1935 Mr. Canty owned the cottage on the top of the hill. That same year there was a devastating fire in 1935 that destroyed it. According to a local newspaper, the fire was noticed by neighbors who tried to fight the fire until the Fire Department arrived. The fire was said to have caused $1,500 in damages and the cottage was unable to be saved and Mr. Canty had to rebuild it.

Thomas Canty became a member in 1915 and remained a member throughout his lifetime. The Canty family lived in Batavia and spent a lot of time in Seven Springs. In September 1935 there was a mention in a local news story of Miss Anna Mae Canty hosting friends from Rochester for the weekend at Seven Springs. The newspaper was published the day before her birthday, and she probably had friends in for a birthday celebration.

Mr. Canty owned this cottage until his death in 1969 when it was transferred to his son Daniel. The cottage remained in the family when it went to Bill and Ken Balling. Billy made his home in the Springs for many years and certainly left his mark on the Club. Billy was usually found in his garden or making a big pot of soup. After his death in 2010, a fundraising campaign was started to raise money for the "Dam Billy" fund to make necessary repairs to the dam. Billy's son Cody took over the cottage in 2010 until it was sold to its current owner Dan Cavalieri. Since 2015 Dan has been working on a complete remodel of the cottage.

There's more to the story of the Canty family. Since 1915 there has been at least one member of the family holding a Seven Springs membership. The Cantys are relatives to the Ballings and to present day member Joan Post. The Canty/Balling/Post family is the longest continuous family having membership in Seven Springs.

CHAPTER 29
Cottage #11

Location: Russell Road (the former location of the Red Raven)
Known as: "Lew Lodge" and "Shangri-La"
Location of the Red Raven

In 1923 Edward McMannis was given permission to build a cottage on Lot #1. Using an original map, containing lot numbers, Lot #1 lines up with cottage 11 (present home of Maddie Ferris). There is not enough documentation to know for sure if this cottage was the original one built by Edward. However, the cottage on that location would eventually be owned by his brother-in-law William Russell. On this spot was the cottage of Seven Springs founder, William ("Billy") Russell.

Known as the Red Raven, Billy Russell's cottage was among the first to be built in the Springs. He owned it for many years before selling it to Adam Ross of Buffalo in 1963. Mr. Ross was an amateur magician and knew Billy through a magician's association that Billy himself started. Adam Ross took down the old cottage and rebuilt it in 1964/65, and this is the current cottage on the site.

By 1969 the cottage was owned by a man named Mr. Ivison who called it "Shangri-La". The Ivison's sold the cottage to Chester Lewandowski in 1973, renaming it the "Lew-Lodge". At one time there was a bridge built from this cottage that went to the Canty's cottage (Cottage #10) The residents would meet in the middle and play cards.

In 1977 the cottage was then sold to Bill Herrington and Delores ("Dee") Bailey who owned it for a number of years. Dee eventually moved to the Springs year-round and lived in the cottage until her death. After her death in 2010 the cottage was purchased by the Club and sold to its current owner Maddie Ferris in 2011. Since then, Maddie has remodeled the cottage and enclosed the side porch.

CHAPTER 30
Cottage #12

Location: Russell Road
Known as: "We Like It"

There are references in early documents to a tent put up on a site by Mr. FA Hovey who was an early member of Seven Springs. Mr. Hovey's membership was eventually sold to John Dorsch. By 1945 the tent had presumably been replaced by a cottage owned by Mr. Dorsch. Much like other cottages in the Springs, the build date doesn't match with the Club's records on cottage #12.

In 1954 the cottage was owned by Howard Peters who sold it in 1958 to John Speidel. The documentation from that year notes that the cottage was called "We Like It". It is possible that the structure on this spot was rebuilt in 1960 to correspond to the county's information. The cottage was owned by Mr. Speidel through the 1960s and was then sold to Ellsworth ("Bus") Bridge in 1971. Bridge sold the cottage to Ginny Sackel in 1978. Ms. Sackel eventually moved away from the area and by 1983 the cottage was purchased by Ricky Lang. Mr. Lang put a 15-foot addition on to the house in 1983. Lang and his family lived there until 1986 when it was sold to Kevin Mancuso. Mr. Mancuso owned the cottage for many years, selling it to Marilyn Torcello in 2007. In 2009 it was purchased by its current occupants, the Tiede family

CHAPTER 31
Cottage #13

Location: Russell Road
Known as: "The Emerald Cottage" and The Green Cottage"

Cottage #13 has a busy history. The earliest mention of a cottage on this spot was in 1923 when it was noted that MJ Tyler was given permission to put up a tent near that of Mr. Hovey (cottage #12). At some point a more permanent structure was built. The Tyler family still owned the cottage in 1945, and by 1954 it had been purchased by John O'Brien. At the time of the purchase the mortgage was held by Mr. Charles Morith. Mr. Morith was in real estate and there were several ads for cottages in the Springs for sale or rent by his agency through the years. His daughter Marjorie became a cottage owner in the Springs as well. During the time that O'Brien owned the cottage an addition to the back was built as well as work done on the foundation.

Mr. O'Brien sold the cottage to Robert Chapman in 1966. In

1969 the cottage was sold again, this time to Virginia Tiede Maas and her husband Clem. They added a roof over the back area. In 1988 Todd Gallup purchased the cottage and by 1989 it was again for sale. The tax assessment list in 1989 identifies Diane Kiecher as the owner. By 1990 the cottage had again changed hands and was then owned by Rubie and Sue Levins. In 1999 the cottage was purchased by its current owner, Greg Post.

Over the years there have been many members who have rented the "Emerald Cottage", some of the past tenants include Allen Greene, Chuck Ward, Rand Fisher, Wayne Younge, and Marcy Crandall. The current resident is Katy Green who has lived there for 3 years.

CHAPTER 32
Cottage #14

Location: Russell Road

Cottage #14 was built by John Radley sometime in 1950. In July of that year there was a complaint of "loud and boisterous conduct" at the cottage - sounds like a great housewarming! By 1954 the cottage had been sold to a Mr. Ernest Netzen. Then, in 1959 Edward R Ferris became a member of Seven Springs and purchased the home. Mr. Ferris is the longest standing member of the Club. The Ferris family lived in this cottage until 1974 when they sold it to Michael and Pam Charvella. The letter "C" chimney adornment was put up by the Charvellas. Mike and Pam are also the godparents of current member Jason Reardon.

In 1978, records show that John Benton was living in the cottage, probably as a rental. Shane and Mary Carver bought the cottage by 1981 and raised their family here. The Carvers did quite a bit of remodeling; additions were put on in 1982 and 1987.

This cottage is currently the longest continuously owned home by the same family.

CHAPTER 33
Cottage #15

Location: Russell Road

The first known owner of Cottage#15 was Myron St. John. He was given permission to build in 1933. In 1945 George Acheson was listed as the owner of this cottage. From there the cottage was sold to Murnis Barton who in turn sold it to Alfred Branton in 1951. Mr. Branton owned the cottage for several years before selling it to Ron and Marge Setzer in 1961. Marge was the daughter of Charles Morith who was a real estate agent who handled several home sales in the Springs. Ron was a teacher in the Batavia school district and was the varsity hockey coach for many years. A 16'x24' addition was put on the home in 1961.

In 1969, the Setzers sold the cottage to a fellow teacher, Mary Kelly. Mary lived in Seven Springs for many years and served on the Board of Directors for several of them. She was an active member and participant dedicated to the betterment of Seven

Springs. An accomplished quilter and avid traveler, Mary added the sun porch in 1981 and also had a pagoda built in 1996. The cottage was then sold to Teresa Ferris and again in 2019 when it was purchased by its current owner Cindy Lewis whose son Andrew lives there.

CHAPTER 34
Cottage #16

Location: Hawkins Hollow Road
Known as: "Kozi Kabin"

The possible first owner of this cottage was Russell Bridge. Bridge was given permission to build on Lot #17 in 1932. The tax assessment roll in 1945 lists the owner of this cottage as Gordon Didus. He owned it for many years until his death in the mid 1970's. The cottage then went to his longtime partner Dorothy Kerr. On the chimney of the house is a stone with "Kozi Kabin" inscribed on it.

In 1976 the cottage was sold to a Mr. Denault and again, later that same year to Don Callan. Mr. Callan was the owner until 1988 when he sold it to Joe and Cheryl Manz. The Manz family lived in the Springs until 1995, at which time the cottage was purchased by Mike Easton. The cottage changed hands again in 1999 when it was sold to Katy Call. Katy put an addition and a deck on the cottage. The cottage was next purchased by Mike and Nancy Pastore in 2011.

Over the years, several tenants have also lived in this cottage including Jim and Kathie Catino and Patty Olverd. The cottage's current occupants are Joe and Chrissy Prucha.

CHAPTER 35
Cottage #17

Hawkins Hollow Road

The first tax assessment list for Seven Springs appeared in 1945. At that time Cottage #17 was owned by Ernie Hawkins. However, the first owner was likely a man named Donald McKenzie, who was given permission to build on Lot #21 in May of 1926. Ernie and his wife Ethel owned the cottage for many years. Ernie was a long-time President and was instrumental in developing and growing Seven Springs.

    The cottage was eventually sold to Bob and Helen Crook in about 1983. Bob was a music teacher in the Batavia School District. The Crooks lived in the city of Batavia before moving into their Springs home year-round. In 1996, they expanded the second story of the cottage. Mr. Crook enjoyed woodworking as a pastime and had a workshop in the basement. Handmade wooden lamps were among his signature pieces, and he would often give one to new neighbors. Mrs. Crook was an artist in her own right, working with photographs, paintings, and fabric. Bob and Helen's daughter Linda eventually moved into the cottage to help her parents. After Helen's death in 2009 the cottage was sold to Mary and Joe Ryan. The Ryan's did a complete remodel on the cottage. The current owners, the Rapones, purchased the home in 2014 and have lived there since with their family.

CHAPTER 36
Cottage #18

Location: Hawkins Hollow Road

Cottage #18's owner on the 1945 tax assessment list was Howard Seeley. Howard and his wife Aldona were longtime members and the original owners of the cottages. Howard grew up on nearby land to the Springs and helped plant trees with Edward Russell as a youth. Mr. Seeley was a city firefighter. He also succeeded Fred Miller as Caretaker and built the gates at the front entrance. There are bricks signed by him along with an inscription of the year it was built (1960). Mr. Seeley died in 1969 and in 1971 the cottage was purchased by Ollie Spaulding. Ollie put an addition on the cottage in 1981. It was approximately that same year that the cottage was sold to Rita Groth in approximately 1981 and she owned it until the early 1990's. In 1994 the cottage was then purchased by its current owners, Cindy and Rick Lewis.

CHAPTER 37
Cottage #19

Location: Hawkins Hollow Road

Documentation shows that Robert Carson became a member in 1927 and was given permission to build Cottage #19 in 1929. Robert Carson was still listed as the cottage owner in 1945, however he died in April of that year after suffering a fall at the cottage. His obituary reads: "Robert T. Carson, who fell downstairs at his Seven Springs cottage died April 2. 1945 aged 65 years, at the Genesee Memorial Hospital. "Mr. Carson worked for P.W. Minor shoe factory and served as President of Seven Springs. His son-in-law, Laverne Peters was also a member of the Springs.

    The cottage was sold to Charles Churchill in 1946. Next, in 1953 the cottage was sold to Walter Schutt Jr and sold again in 1954 to Ronald Carnahan who later transferred it to his father George. The Carnahans owned the cottage for until 1981, at which time Maddie Della Penna Ferris then purchased it. Maddie and Eddie lived there until 1987, when they moved to a house on the main road and sold the cottage to Marcia Derck. Ms. Derck then sold it to the Tenney family in 1996 who sold it to its current owner David Wicks in 1998.

CHAPTER 38
Cottage #20

Location: Hawkins Hollow Road
Known as the "Pink Candle"

Louis Grundler was listed as the owner of Cottage #20 in 1945. He owned it until 1957 when it was sold to Andrew McWain Jr. Mr. McWain's father was the longtime owner and editor of the *Batavia Daily News*. In 1961, The cottage was sold to Eugene Trout. Mr. Trout owned it until 1976, selling it to Anna Mae Balling. Anna Mae's father was Thomas Canty who was an early member and cottage owner in the Springs.

Anna Mae was a character, with her snowy white hair and twinkle in her eyes, and the Pink Candle, as it came to be known was always open to a friend for a beverage and a chat. Anna Mae was a nurse and the mother of eight children, so she certainly earned her retirement in the little cottage in the Springs. In 1995 the cottage was purchased by its current owner and Anna Mae's daughter, Joan Post. Although currently unoccupied, Joan had rented the cottage to Greg Dermody for some time.

CHAPTER 39
Cottage #21

Location: Seven Springs Road

The earliest listed owner for this cottage was Francis Kennedy in 1954. Club records show that there was a structure built on this spot around 1949. Like several other cottages, the county records don't match exactly to club records. Mr. Kennedy was employed at Doehler Jarvis and was involved with local politics. During the time he owned the cottage he attempted to sell it several times.

The first sale was in 1956. There was no explanation in club records as to why the cottage went back in Kennedy's name by 1957. In 1958, a man had agreed to buy it and attained club membership, but he changed his mind when he found out he couldn't run water to the cottage. In 1961 the cottage was again sold, however they failed to notify the Board and the new owner's membership was not approved. Finally, later that same year, the cottage was sold to Vernon Carnahan. Mr. Carnahan's brother, Gordon also later became a cottage owner in the Springs (Cottage #19). A newspaper mention of Mr. Carnhan selling his home on Trumbull Parkway that says he "contemplates building". Most likely this cottage was rebuilt in 1962. After Vern's death, his wife Florence took over the cottage and membership, followed by their daughter Jean Smith. Next, the cottage was sold in around 1987/88 to Eddie and Maddie Ferris. They put an addition on to the home in 1992. The cottage was then sold to the current owner Andrew Ferris and his family.

CHAPTER 40
Cottage #22

Location: Seven Springs Road

Cottage #22 has the distinction of being one of two homes that are built along the main Seven Springs Rd. It is also the only cottage that is still occupied by its original owner and builder. Built in 1987, this cottage is the third one to be owned by Mr. Ferris. Mr. Ferris lives there with his wife Mary Jane and daughter, Lori. Now in his 90's, Mr. Ferris is still an active member of the Springs. Most days he is seen taking a walk through the property and often helps with projects around the neighborhood.

CHAPTER 41
O'Brien Cottage

Location: No longer exists

This cottage was located next to Cottage #14 (present-day Mary Carver's home) and across from the Cottage #7 (currently the Reardon's home), but no longer exists. Records show that in 1945 the owner was Herbert Smith, who was probably a relative of MJ Smith, owner of a nearby cottage. Herbert was given permission to build the cottage in 1927. By 1954 the cottage was owned by the Stroh's, while their daughter and son-in-law (Reigle) owned the cottage across the road (now the Reardon's). The Stroh family sold the cottage in about 1959/60. A note found in Club records show that Albert Stroh asked to sell his membership in 1959 and give the proceeds to his daughter Mrs. Evelyn Riegle.

The new owner of the cottage, Leo O'Brien was the father of John O'Brien who was a long-time member of Seven Springs. After Leo's death in 1964 the cottage went to his wife Delores. Delores was the daughter of John and Mary Ann Francis Kenney. The Francis family owned several acres on the corner of Seven Springs

Road and Route 5 as part of a larger farm, and they donated 15 acres of this land to Seven Springs.

Delores went on to remarry Mr. Julius Stein and lived to the age of 99. In 1970 John O'Brien was listed as the cottage owner; however, over time the cottage had fallen into disrepair and was knocked down that same year. ↓

SECTION IX

Everything Else

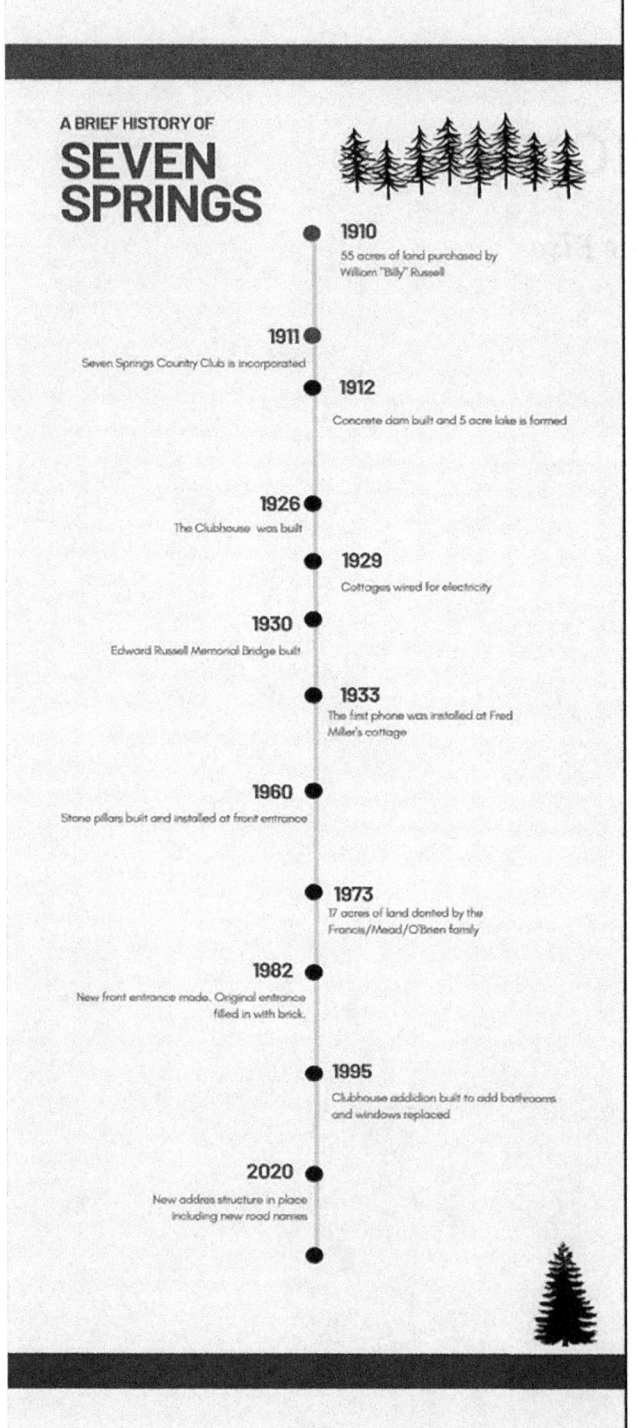

Seven Springs Fun Facts

The longest current member is Ed Ferris. He has been a member since 1956!

The Ferris family has more members than any other family

 Seven Springs Cottages have on average 5.6 owners

The cottage with the MOST owners is Cottage #12 Owned by The Tiedes

The cottage with the LEAST owners is Cottage #22 Owned by Ed Ferris

Seven Springs Country Club

CHAPTER 42
Water

One of Seven Springs finest assets is its clear, crisp beautiful water. Since the time before the Europeans arrived and formed boundaries, the natural springs were well known to the native people. Even then the area was known as a place to come for fresh, clean water and plentiful hunting and fishing. It was believed that at one time there were actually seven springs here. Through repeated freezing and thawing, the growth of tree roots, and even earthquakes, numerous other springs were brought to the surface. There is documentation of several named springs including: Alpha, Tyler's Amphitheatre, and Bergman

Longtime caretaker Fred Miller reported one such earthquake that occurred in the early hours one morning. Mr. Miller could not remember exactly when the earthquake occurred but recalled that it was not felt as strongly in Batavia as it was toward Attica. In a 1952 interview with the *Batavia Daily News* Mr. Miller said the following about the changes that occurred due to the earthquake: "When I selected the spot for my cabin 33 years ago, I looked carefully and found a site that was absolutely dry. Later came this quake, which shook and rattled the house. After the shaking was over, I had a spring right in the middle of my cellar. I've had lots of water there since.". An earlier article about Mr. Miller in 1946 mentions that the spring below his house provided water for his sink.

It may be surprising to learn that Seven Springs and the surrounding area very nearly became a bottling plant. In 1902 two companies out of New York planned to purchase the Gardner Farm and surrounding area. The news reported that a large plant would be built and that the water from the springs would be purified using an electrical process. They described the purchase of Gardner Farm stating the land "on which the famous Seven Springs are located with the mill and water rights connected with the property". It is unknown why the sale of the farm and surrounding land was not completed but fortunately the land was left alone until the Seven Springs Club was formed.

Water rights were first granted to an original member, Mr. Charles Buxton. He built a pump house that resembled a cabin. The filtered water was sold to the public. The pump house burned down in 1914 and was not rebuilt. The Batavia Pure Ice and Water company also held water rights for some time.

In the 1920's water rights were sold to another member, Mr. William Gamble. Gamble used the water to make soft drinks, with many advertisements noting the use of the excellent Seven Springs water. Mr. Gamble's process included adding chlorine and then running the water through a series of filters to take out any impurities. A former employee, Jon McManis said that when he worked for the company in the 1950s, he came to the Springs every morning to fill the tanker truck. The truck held 750 gallons, and, upon filling the truck, he drove it to the Gamble plant on Elm Street in Batavia for use in making soft drinks. The truck was filled from a pump housed in a wooden box, a pipe ran up the side of a tree and had a large diameter hose that was used to fill the tanker. Mr. McManis mentioned how much he enjoyed his morning trips to the property and often saw wildlife while filling the truck.

After Mr. Gamble, water rights were held for a time by Mr. Richard Lyman.

Today, residents as well as members who do not live in Seven Springs still take advantage of the fresh spring water by filling jugs from a faucet near the Clubhouse.

CHAPTER 43
The Strange, the Unusual and the Sometimes Sad

As a neighborhood Seven Springs is home to a unique and lovely group of people. Throughout the years residents have come from all walks of life and backgrounds: businesspeople and artists, families and those living on their own. While it may seem like a perhaps quirky mix of people, everyone shares in their love of the beautiful woods, trails, and water. It would seem that our inherent quirkiness has been handed down through the years. What follows is a collection of stories that is strange, unusual, and sometimes sad.

Ensigns Hollow
In the early years before Seven Springs was formed the land was owned by a Mr. Seymour Ensign. An article from the *Sunday Times* tells the story as follows; "A good many years ago, a woolen mill was located here, operated by waterpower from the pond and was owned by a man named Ensign. There are many stories about Ensign's belief in witchcraft. Tradition says that Ensign, through his connection with witches, was told that treasure in great amount was buried somewhere in the hills surrounding the pond. Ensign

was a clairvoyant, and it was said was able to go into a trance and receive messages. Among these messages was one telling him about the buried treasure. He had hard luck however, for he would hardly regain his senses after one of his trances before the witches would remove the chest of gold to some other place. But so strong was Ensign's belief, that he spent much of his time after dark digging among the hills. Each night he would take a lantern and spend several hours digging in first one and then another but always failing to find the hiding place. To bear out the story of the digging, there can be seen even now, hummocks and holes where it is said Ensign had been digging.". It is likely that the mill mentioned in the article was a grist mill located at the present-day Chapin Mill.

Beyond the story in this article Seymour Ensign is somewhat of a mystery. He was not the original owner of the property and records exist showing that he owned property in the Medina area also. The exact years in which Ensign owned the property are unknown. However, there is documentation that beginning around 1850 the pond at Chapin Mills was known as Gardner's Pond, it was called this well into the 1900s. Earlier in the 1800s the general area was called Ensign's Hollow, but no further information was able to be found about Mr. Ensign.

The Sad Tale of George Grentzinger
The following gruesome news story appeared in a Washington DC newspaper in 1896.

There was also an article that appeared in *The Buffalo News* regarding this sad story. Mr. Grentzinger's death was ruled a suicide. The article mentioned that he had been missing for several days and his body was only found after a clairvoyant from Perry, NY had been consulted. An early Batavia newspaper entitled *The Batavian* reported that the 29-year-old machinist had been suffering from an illness known as "despondency". He was survived by his wife and is buried in the Elmwood Cemetery in Batavia.

Stolen Goods

In 1914 a father and daughter took a walk through Seven Springs and discovered a treasure trove of ladies' shoes and bolts of fabrics. Police were summoned and the goods were linked to a string of recent burglaries from local railroads. Two men were arrested, and the robbery ring was broken up.

Lost Fish

The following story of a lost fish appeared in June of 1915 in the *Batavia Daily News* and is best presented in its entirety: "There is a sequel to the recent catching of the huge brown trout by William H. Moran at Seven Springs, which he is not relating with the same degree of pride as he did the catch. After landing the fish, Mr. Moran prepared a nice bed of watercress and laid the fish on it in a basket. On reaching home he was surprised to find the fish was gone. He called up President Russell of the Seven Springs Club and procured lanterns and a rig and went back to the springs hot foot. After a search the fish was found intact in the grass near where the basket had been set. It appeared that a tame goat had been in the vicinity and tipped over the basket".

The first part of the story alluded in the opening of the article was not found, however more research did reveal that Mr. Moran was a long-time employee of the Daily News. The article was probably written with some good-natured teasing by his co-workers.

Railroad Detective Shot

A much more frightening event occurred in August of 1915. A detective with the Lehigh Valley Railroad, named McCormick was shot while in pursuit of a suspect. The suspect fled into the Seven Springs woods. Detective McCormick had been shot in the upper left side of his nose and required emergency surgery to remove a ball lodged behind his right eye. Remarkably, Detective McCormick survived the surgery, and his eye was not damaged. An extensive search was conducted throughout the Seven Springs property, but the suspect was not found. The *Batavia Daily News* reported that the incident began "when he attempted to question a man whom he met walking along the tracks just east of the Lehigh crossing on East Main Street Road".

Authorities believed the man was involved in an attack of a mother and daughter. Eventually Mr. Jan Trybus was arrested and tried for the attacks and the shooting of Detective McCormick as well as the shooting of another railroad detective.

Captain Ryan's Company
1917- Another unusual headline was found from *The Daily News* October 15, 1917. "Captain Ryan's Company Walked to Seven Springs". The article told of a home defense regiment, thirty in number, who marched together from Russell Place in Batavia to Seven Springs in forty-five minutes. Once at the property they split into two squads and were led by "Privates Russell and Tyler" to inspect the grounds.

Car Accidents
A car accident occurred within the Springs property in 1926 the newspaper reported that a Miss Martha Ferry was driving her sedan on the north road of the grounds. The driver backed up and slid off a bank causing the car to tip over on its side. Miss Ferry was accompanied by Miss Anna MacKenzie and three younger children. No one was seriously injured, but the car was reportedly heavily damaged.

At that time Mr. Donald MacKenzie was a Club member and Anna was likely a relative of Donald. Researching the census records did not help to connect them but did reveal that Mr. Mackenzie was employed by the *Batavia Daily News*. He was initially listed as married but living on his own as a boarder, and by the next census he was listed as divorced. The Mackenzie family seemed to have had bad luck on the property's road. Donald himself had an accident in 1937. The newspaper reported that he hit a tree after he "lost control of the car on the narrow road when his foot slipped from the brake pedal to the accelerator". He suffered cuts and bruises and was treated at St. Jerome's Hospital.

Squirrels

In 1927 the Club was plagued with an unknown animal that was causing damage to pine trees on the property. Approximately 50 Scotch pine trees were killed by an unknown, "mysterious" animal. According to the article in the *Batavia Daily News* the trees located near the Erie railroad tracks were being damaged by an animal that was eating chunks of bark from the upper branches. The animal would eat the bark in rings from the top down, eventually killing the trees. President Miller, Melvin Tyler, and Fred Miller went so far as to stakeout the area overnight for several nights to no avail. The climax of the mystery was reported as follows: "Sunday afternoon Mr. Miller saw an animal, which he thinks was an opossum, in the vicinity of the grove. Hastening to his home he obtained his shotgun, but the animal had disappeared by the time he returned. Yesterday afternoon, however, Mr. Miller had his gun with him and saw the animal at a distance. He shot at long range and the animal dropped, but when he reached the spot there was no animal there." The article went on to report that even though the animal was not found, no further damage occurred to the trees after the incident.

Even though it seemed that the mystery had been solved, five days after the original article, another article appeared in the *Buffalo Courier*. In the second article Fred Miller was said to have witnessed the damage being done firsthand. The culprit was, in fact, a red squirrel. The Club caretaker vowed to wage war on the devious squirrels.

However, the saga of squirrels in Seven Springs was not yet done.

An article in the *Batavia Daily News* published in January 1929 told of damage done to Mr. MacKenzie's cottage. The news reported that Mr. MacKenzie returned to "his shack" after being out of town for a couple of weeks to find chaos. "Things being strewn about the rooms and dishes and bric-a-brac thrown from shelves and broken". The damage was inflicted by gray squirrels this time, who along with making a large mess, cleaned the cottage out of anything edible. They found a paper sack of nuts, broke it open

and made off with the contents, leaving only a trail of shells. The article went on to say the following: "They tried to carry away a loaf of hard bread, but they could not get it out of the shack, and it was stuck fast in a crack." Apparently, the squirrels had planted some of the nuts under two pillows on a couch but had later carried them away leaving a few outside shells under the pillows."
On a personal note (and for full disclosure), the writer of this book has an abject dislike of squirrels and would be pleased to share more stories showcasing their true devious nature.

A Break In
One evening in March 1933, Supt. Fred Miller discovered a break in along with a man, sleeping in the cottage of Myron St John. The police were called, and the following report appeared in the *Batavia Times*. "John Shaer, 68, homeless, was arrested by State Police on a charge of disorderly conduct when he was found lying in a cottage at Seven Springs in a paralyzed condition as a result of drinking denatured alcohol". Mr. Shafer pleaded guilty and spent 10 days in jail.

Earthquake
As mentioned earlier, there were documented reports of earthquakes affecting the Seven Springs area. One such occurrence happened in November 1935. A small earthquake was felt in both Batavia and Alexander. The article in *The Times* reported the incident from the viewpoint of Supt. Miller. "What seemed to be the best report came from Fred Miller, caretaker of the Seven Spring Country Club." Fred described how hundreds of pheasants roosting on the property were awoken by three shocks, saying "the pheasants squawked as soon as the quake started, and they kept it up for three-quarters of an hour afterwards". He continued by saying "It was the third quake I've felt here, but this is low ground, close to the rock and they're more noticeable here than on the high lands." The article ends by reporting that no damage was done as a result of the quake.

Woodchuck Hollow

1939 - Many years ago the area near Seven Springs (where the Mason family built their homes) was known as "Woodchuck Hollow". It was a popular spot for area residents to ski and sled. The hollow is quite steep and before it was filled in with trees it was probably a very good spot for winter sports. There were a few articles in the local newspapers mentioning afternoon trips to Woodchuck Hollow. An article written in February of 1939 in the *Batavia Daily News* tells of a serious accident; "Two young women are in St. Jerome's Hospital with injuries suffered yesterday afternoon when thrown from a toboggan on their first trip down a hill at Woodchuck Hollow near Seven Springs. They are Miss Ruth Meier, 23 of Morganville, back injuries the extent of which were to be determined with an X-ray examination and Miss Gertrude McClure, 27, of No 14 Franklin Street who suffered a fractured jaw". The women were with a group of ten people and none of the others were injured seriously.

Don't Pick the Flowers

In 1952 - An article written by J.E. Brown in the Batavia Daily News discussed the growing number of signs appearing throughout Batavia and the surrounding area. The article went on to describe some of the signage in the Springs. "There's one in particular on the Seven Springs Country Club property a couple of miles east of Batavia. That section is owned by lovers of the outdoors and is not open to the public. The wooded area that contains a lake, has cottages, and provides spring drinking water has some new signs, the product, they say, of the magic brush of William A. Russell, himself a cottager at the scenic spot. The owners take considerable pride in the nature areal and keep the many acres spick and span and close as possible to the way nature made them. Near one of the spring-fed streams, is this small sign that issues in red letter, this sensible reminder: Do Not Pick Wildflowers. God Placed Them Where They Look Best".

Very sensible advice indeed.

Tornado

1993 - On September 3, 1993, a category-one tornado touched down near Seven Springs. The roof was torn off a nearby house and carried for a quarter of a mile. The force of the tornado lifted a delivery truck onto a tractor trailer, both drivers were killed. For months after the accident items from the trucks were found scattered through the woods surrounding the area.

* * *

Seven Springs Country Club is a unique, secluded spot that has played an important role in Genesee County's history throughout the years. It is a testament to the beauty of conservation but even more importantly it is a community of neighbors. Seven Springs has grown and flourished over the last 110 years and none of it would have been possible without its residents and members. The vision of its founders has come to life with years of hard work and stewardship. Today's members continue to honor the land, by planting new trees and caring for the property. This is done with the hope that the next generation will take up the mantle and continue the work.

REFERENCES

Section I

Conklin, Susan. Genesee County Timeline. Retrieved September 16, 2021, from https://www.co.genesee.ny.us/departments/history/genesee_county_time_line.php

Dam Went Out. (1951, September 6). *The Batavia Daily News*. Page 23. Retrieved from: Fulton history.

Gazetteer and Biographical on Genesee County, N.Y. 1788-1890.

Oral History as told to Andres Chapin. (2019). Received from Rochester Zen Center.

Trietley, Virginia. Progress Cut Fanciful Capers in Godfrey Pond Transition; Great Time When

Very Personal. (1935, September 12). The Batavia Times. Page 4. Retrieved from Fulton history

Section II

Articles of Incorporation Seven Springs Country Club. (1911, July 14). *The Batavia Daily News*. Page seven. Retrieved from: https://fultonhistory.com/Fulton.html

Country Club to Build Clubhouse. (1914, October 25). *The Sunday Times*. Page 1. Retrieved from: https://fultonhistory.com/Fulton.html

Seven Springs Country Club. (1910, October 25). Meeting of the Board of Directors, SSCC files, Batavia, NY.

Seven Springs Country Club. (1911, March 10). Meeting of the Board of Directors, SSCC files, Batavia, NY.

Seven Springs Country Club. (1911, September 11). Meeting of the Board of Directors, SSCC files, Batavia, NY.

Seven Springs Country Club. (1921, April 10). Meeting of the Board of Directors, SSCC files, Batavia, NY.

Seven Springs Country Club. (1923, July). Meeting of the Board of Directors, SSCC files, Batavia, NY.

Seven Springs Country Club. (1911, March 11). *The Batavia Daily News*. Retrieved from: https://fultonhistory.com/Fulton.html

Seven Springs Work. (1912, March 31). *The Sunday Times.* Retrieved from: https://fultonhistory.com/Fulton.html

Six-Acre Lake Formed by Man. (1912, August 7). *The Batavia Daily News.* Page six. Retrieved from: https://fultonhistory.com/Fulton.html

Unknown author. Brief history. Original copy held by Genesee County History Department. Retrieved: August 2021.

Work at Seven Springs. (1912, January 21). *The Sunday Times.* Page 1. Retrieved from: https://fultonhistory.com/Fulton.html

Section III

Batavia High School. (1931). *The Batavian* [Yearbook]. Ancestry.com

Brown, J.E., Earliest Films Recalled. (1954, January 31). *The Batavia Daily News.* Page 2. Retrieved from: https://fultonhistory.com/Fulton.html

Brown, J.E. Warm Turn Seen at Hand. (1956, May 24). *The Batavia Daily News.* Page 2. **Retrieved from:** https://fultonhistory.com/Fulton.html

Early Days of the "Flickers" Recalled by Theatre Opening. (1947, April 17). *The Batavia Daily News.* Page six. Retrieved from: https://fultonhistory.com/Fulton.html

F.E. Russell Dies at 88. (1966, March 3). *The Batavia Daily News.* Page 4. Retrieved from: https://fultonhistory.com/Fulton.html

Find a Grave. https://www.findagrave.com/memorial/80189258/thomas-c-canty

Fred Miller, 96, Weather Prophet, Dies. (1960, January 30). *Buffalo Courier-Express.* Page 19. **Retrieved from:** https://fultonhistory.com/Fulton.html

Fred F Miler, Sage Dies at 96. (1960, January 30). *Democrat and Chronicle.* Page 9. Retrieved from Newspapers.com October 10, 2021

Marriage at Batavia in St. Joseph Church of Two Popular Young People. (1903, August 20). *Democrat and Chronicle.* Rochester, NY. Page 5. Retrieved from: https://fultonhistory.com/Fulton.html

McAvoy, Ruth M. A History of the City of Batavia. 974.792 MCEV, pg. 62. Held by Richmond Memorial Library.

Miss Russell Dead, Teacher, Dramatist. (1953, November). *The Batavia Daily News.* Page 4. Retrieved from: https://fultonhistory.com/Fulton.html

N.Y. State (1925). State Census. Retrieved from https://www.ancestry.com/discoveryui-content/view/23863890:2704?ssrc=pt&tid=163970266&pid=402324633212

Obituaries. Edward Russell. (1971, January 18). *The Batavia Daily News.* Page 4. Retrieved from: https://fultonhistory.com/Fulton.html

Obituaries. Mrs. Edward McMannis. (1976, October 5). *The Batavia Daily News.* Page 4. Retrieved from: https://fultonhistory.com/Fulton.html

Obituaries Thomas Canty. (1967). *The Batavia Daily News.* Retrieved from: Retrieved from: https://fultonhistory.com/Fulton.html

Obituaries. (2005, January 1). *The Buffalo News.* Retrieved from Ancestry.com

Personal. (1926, Feb 5). *The Batavia Daily News.* Page 6. Retrieved from: https://fultonhistory.com/Fulton.html

Seven Springs Caretaker Enjoying Life in Scenic Spot. (1946, August 31). *The Batavia Daily News.* Page 8. Retrieved from: https://fultonhistory.com/Fulton.html

Seven Springs Club Tract Model of Reforesting and Game Haven. (1928, April 22). *Democrat and Chronicle.* Copy retrieved from Genesee County History Department.

U.S. Census Bureau (1860). Federal Census. Ancestry.com. Retrieved from https://www.ancestry.com/family-tree/person/tree/177027835/person/112302839316/hints?Hints.hintStatus=pending&successSource=Hint&_phtarg=XtA775&msg=ntm&msgParams=%7c1%7c1%7c&mpid=112302839316&shid=1037939923121&nec=1&mdbid=60525&mrpid=32299098

U.S. Census Bureau (1880). Federal Census. Retrieved from https://www.ancestry.com/imageviewer/collections/6742/images/4242168-00293?pId=3415784

U.S. Census Bureau (1880). Federal Census. Retrieved from https://www.ancestry.com/discoveryui-content/view/39474873:6742?ssrc=pt&tid=178461238&pid=422321854274

U.S. Census Bureau (1900). Federal Census. Retrieved from https://www.ancestry.com/discoveryui-content/view/66211367:7602?ssrc=pt&tid=178461238&pid=422321854274

U.S. Census Bureau (1900). Federal Census. Retrieved from https://www.ancestry.com/imageviewer/collections/7602/images/4114521_00069?pId=66213345

U.S. Census Bureau (1910). Federal Census. Retrieved from https://www.ancestry.com/discoveryui-content/view/140032686:7884?ssrc=pt&tid=178461238&pid=422321854274

U.S. Census Bureau (1920). Federal Census. Ancestry.com. Retrieved from https://www.ancestry.com/imageviewer/collections/6061/images/4313446-00138?pId=90873112

U.S. Census Bureau (1920). Federal Census. Ancestry.com Retrieved from https://www.ancestry.com/family-tree/person/tree/178709060/person/382326092042/hints

U.S. Census Bureau (1930). Federal Census. Ancestry.com Retrieved from https://www.ancestry.com/family-tree/person/tree/178709060/person/382326091380/hints

U.S. Census Bureau (1940). Federal Census. Ancestry.com. Retrieved from https://www.ancestry.com/imageviewer/collections/2442/images/m-t0627-02538-00366?pId=6764922

U.S., Find a Grave Index, 1600's-Current. (2012). Ancestry.com. https://www.ancestry.com/discoveryui-content/view/90731260:60525?ssrc=pt&tid=178709060&pid=382326091380

U.S. Census Bureau (1920). Federal Census. Ancestry.com. Retrieved from https://www.ancestry.com/imageviewer/collections/6061/images/4313446-00138?pId=90873112

Western N.Y. to have a Mild Winter. (1954, November 29). *The Evening Telegram*, Herkimer, N.Y. Page 7. Retrieved from: https://fultonhistory.com/Fulton.html

Section IV

250 Western New Yorkers to See Reforestation Work. (1929, June 3). *Buffalo Evening News*. Retrieved from: https://fultonhistory.com/Fulton.html

Dromgoole, Will Allen (1931). "The Bridge Builder". Poetry Foundation.org

Wikipedia. Retrieved September 5, 2021.

New Road at Seven Springs. (1914, July 27). *The Batavia Daily News*. Page 4. Retrieved from: https://fultonhistory.com/

Fulton.html
Reforestation. (1922. February 15). Leroy Gazette-News. Retrieved from: https://fultonhistory.com/Fulton.html
Reforestation of Batavia Tract Largely the Work of Hoboes. (1929, May 1). *Buffalo Evening News.* Retrieved from: https://fultonhistory.com/Fulton.html
Seven Springs Bridge Formally Dedicated, Officers Re-Elected. (1930, May 31). *The Batavia Daily News.* Page six. Retrieved from: https://fultonhistory.com/Fulton.html
Seven Springs Club's Property to Have Gates. (1923, May 15). *The Batavia Daily News.* Page 1. Retrieved from: https://fultonhistory.com/Fulton.html
Seven Spring Club Cornerstone in Place. (1929. October 16). *The Batavia Daily News.* Retrieved from: https://fultonhistory.com/Fulton.html.
Seven Springs Club's Elections. (1923, June 2). *The Batavia Daily News.* Page 5. Retrieved from: https://fultonhistory.com/Fulton.html
Seven Springs Concrete Dam. (1912, August 31). *The Times* Batavia, New York. https://fultonhistory.com/Fulton.html
Seven Springs Dam Fine Piece of Work. (1912, October 29). *Batavia Daily News.* Retrieved from https://fultonhistory.com/Fulton.html.
Seven Springs Lake Referred to as a Gem. (1913, April 26). *Batavia Daily News.* Retrieved from https://fultonhistory.com/Fulton.html.
Seven Springs Reforestation. (1921. April 29). *The Batavia Daily News.* Page 7. Retrieved from: https://fultonhistory.com/Fulton.html
Seven Springs Country Club 1960 July Board meeting
Seven Springs Country Club May 26, 1932, annual meeting

Section V

All Around Town. (1927 August 27). *The Batavia Times.* Page 1. Retrieved from https://fultonhistory.com/Fulton.html.
Batavia. (1910, July 25). *Buffalo Evening News.* Retrieved from: https://www.newspapers.com/clip/85925750/marriage-of-mary-elizabeth-mcmanus
Batavia Man Meets Death in Club Pond. (1934, December 14). *The Rochester Democrat and Chronicle.* Page 26. Retrieved from https://

fultonhistory.com/Fulton.html.

Funeral Services Largely Attended. (1934, December). *The Batavia Daily News*. Retrieved from https://fultonhistory.com/Fulton.html.

Gold Rush Era Recalled here at a Reunion. (1937 March 4). *The Batavia Times*. Page 1. Retrieved from https://fultonhistory.com/Fulton.html.

Gold Rush Miners to Klondike will have Annual Meet. (1944 April 20). *The Batavia Times*. Retrieved from https://fultonhistory.com/Fulton.html.

Italian Class Students Greatly Enjoyed Picnic. (1915 May 14). *The Batavia Daily News*. Page five. Retrieved from https://fultonhistory.com/Fulton.html.

Late Local News Items. (1931, May 7). *The Times*, Batavia, NY. Retrieved from https://fultonhistory.com/Fulton.html.Owen, Howard. Quite the Ceremony Reported on Seven

Lions Club Taking Children to Contest. (1957 August 6). *The Batavia Daily News*. Page four. Retrieved from https://fultonhistory.com/Fulton.html.

Outing of Fish and Game Men. (1913 August 24). *The Sunday Times*. Retrieved from https://fultonhistory.com/Fulton.html.

Owen, Howard. Quite the Ceremony Reported on Seven Springs Road. (2012, July 19). The Batavian. Retrieved from: https://www.thebatavian.com/howard-owens/quite-ceremony-reported-seven-springs-road/32952

Personal. (1929 October 31). *The Batavia Daily News*. Page six. Retrieved from https://fultonhistory.com/Fulton.html.

Seven Springs Club Clambake. (1911, September 7). *The Batavia Daily News*. Retrieved from https://fultonhistory.com/Fulton.html.

Seven Springs Cottager Died in the Water. (1934, December 13). *The Batavia Daily News*. Retrieved from https://fultonhistory.com/Fulton.html.

Seven Springs Country Club. (1925, May). Meeting of the Board of Directors, Book held by Ed Ferris, Batavia, NY.

Seven Springs Country Club. (1926, January). Meeting of the Board of Directors, Book held by Ed Ferris, Batavia, NY.

Seven Springs Country Club. (1931, May). Meeting of the Board of Directors, Book held by Ed Ferris, Batavia, NY.

Seven Springs Country Club. (1932, May). Meeting of the Board of Directors, Book held by Ed Ferris, Batavia, NY.

Seven Springs Country Club (1939, July 20). *The Batavia Times.* Page 7. Retrieved from https://fultonhistory.com/Fulton.html.
Seven Springs Fire Caught in Time. (1912, July 13). *The Batavia Daily News.* Retrieved from https://fultonhistory.com/Fulton.html.
Seven Springs Fire Destroys Cottage. (1935, unknown date). *The Times* Batavia, New York. Retrieved from https://fultonhistory.com/Fulton.html.
Seven Springs Lake Referred to as a Gem. (1913, April 26). *The Batavia Daily News.* Retrieved from https://fultonhistory.com/Fulton.html.
Social News Organizations. (1930, August 16). *The Buffalo Evening News.* Page 10. Retrieved from https://fultonhistory.com/Fulton.html.
Society News (1933, August 17). *The Batavia Times.* Page Five. Retrieved from https://fultonhistory.com/Fulton.html.
Society of Artists Plans Outing Sunday. (1959, June). *The Batavia Daily News.* Page 7. Retrieved from https://fultonhistory.com/Fulton.html.
Women's League Picnic Ground (1919, July 10). *The Batavia Daily News.* Retrieved from https://fultonhistory.com/Fulton.html.

Section VII

Mason Family Tree 1600-2018. Book received from John Bertrand and family.
Genesee County New York. Retrieved from: https://genesee.nygenweb.net/Stafford/Stafford%20-%20Home.htm
Two Homes Will be Erected by Mason Family. (1937, March 4). *The Batavia Times.* Page 1. Retrieved from https://fultonhistory.com/Fulton.html.
Very Personal. (1935, September 12). *The Batavia Times.* Page 4. Retrieved from https://fultonhistory.com/Fulton.html.

Section IX

A Clairvoyant's Lucky Hit. (1896, December 13). *The Buffalo Courier*. Page 18. Retrieved from: https://fultonhistory.com/Fulton.html

Automobile Tipped Over. (1926. July 31). *The Batavia Daily News*. Page three. Retrieved from: https://fultonhistory.com/Fulton.html

Bottling Concern at Seven Springs. (1902, October 4). *The Batavia Daily News*. Page 1. Retrieved from: https://fultonhistory.com/Fulton.html

Brown, J.E., These are Days for Some Signs. (1952, April 26). *The Batavia Daily News.* Page two. Retrieved from: https://fultonhistory.com/Fulton.html

Captain Ryan's Company Walked to Seven Springs. (1917, October 15). *The Batavia Daily* News. Page six. Retrieved from: https://fultonhistory.com/Fulton.html

Country Club to Build Clubhouse. (1914, October 25). *The Sunday Times*. Retrieved from: https://fultonhistory.com/Fulton.html

D.B. McKenzie Hurt When Car Hit a Tree. (1937, July 10). *The Batavia Daily News*. Page seven. Retrieved from: https://fultonhistory.com/Fulton.html

Detective McCormick Shot Down. (1915, August 12). *The Batavia Daily News*. Page ten. Retrieved from: https://fultonhistory.com/Fulton.html

Earthquakes, Acts of Nature Boost Seven Springs to 100; Water has High Purity Rating. (1952, January 19). *The Batavia Daily News.* Retrieved from Genesee County History Department.

Goods Hidden at Seven Springs. (1914). *The Times*. Batavia, NY. Retrieved from: https://fultonhistory.com/Fulton.html

Head Nearly Severed. (1896, December 9) *The Morning times*. Page 2. Retrieved from: https://fultonhistory.com/Fulton.html

Insane From Sickness. (1896, December 11). *The Batavian.* Page 1. Retrieved from: https://fultonhistory.com/Fulton.html

Late Local News Items. (1933, March 30). *The Batavia Times*. Page Five. Retrieved from: https://fultonhistory.com/Fulton.html

Mysterious Animal Damaged Pine Trees at Seven Springs. (1927 June, 21). *The Batavia Daily* News. Page twelve. Retrieved from: https://fultonhistory.com/Fulton.html

Officers Arrested Suspects. (1915, October 28). *The Batavia Daily News*. Page seven. Retrieved from: https://fultonhistory.com/Fulton.html

Oral History interview with Jon McMannis. Oral History as told to

Mary Ellen Reardon (2021 September).

Past and Present. (1929, January 12). *The Batavia Daily News.* Page five. Retrieved from: https://fultonhistory.com/Fulton.html

Seven Spring Beverages. (1930, July18). *The Batavia Daily News.* Page 6. Retrieved from: https://fultonhistory.com/Fulton.html

Seven Springs Caretaker Enjoying Life in Scenic Spot. (1946, August 31). *The Batavia Daily News.* Page 8. Retrieved from: https://fultonhistory.com/Fulton.html

Slight Quake Felt by Light Sleepers. (1935, November 7). *The Batavia Times.* Page four. Retrieved from: https://fultonhistory.com/Fulton.html

The Past and Present. (1915, June 26). *The Batavia Daily News.* Page five. Retrieved from: https://fultonhistory.com/Fulton.html

Solve Tree Mystery. (1927, June 26). *The Buffalo Courier.* Retrieved from Fulton history

Tornadoes have been rare in GLOW region. (2021, September 22). *The Daily News Online.* Retrieved from: https://www.thedailynewsonline.com/news/tornadoes-have-been-rare-in-glow-region/article_662e580c-375f-5471-8532-13453e912f32.html

Two Young Women Suffered Injuries in Toboggan Smash. (1939, February 13). *The Batavia Daily News.* Page 1. Retrieved from: https://fultonhistory.com/Fulton.html

Other References

Andrew J. McWain, 88, Dies, Editor of the Batavia Daily News. (1949, March 6). *The Democrat and Chronicle.* https://www.newspapers.com/image/135508610/?terms=andrew%20mcwain&match=1

Batavian buys Carnahan Property. (1962, April 13). *The Batavia Daily News.* Retrieved from: https://fultonhistory.com/Fulton.html

Country Club at Springs Building in the Grove. (1925, July 6). *The Batavia Daily News.* Retrieved from https://fultonhistory.com/Fulton.html.

Deaths, Robert Carson. (1945, April 5). *The Batavia Times.* Page 5. Retrieved from https://fultonhistory.com/Fulton.html.

Late Local News Items. (1931, May 7). *The Batavia Times.* Retrieved from https://fultonhistory.com/Fulton.html.

Oral History interviews with Ed Ferris. Oral History as told to Mary Ellen Reardon (2019, 2020, 2021).

Oral History interviews with Mary Carver. Oral History as told to Mary Ellen Reardon (2020, 2021).

Oral History interviews with Madeline Ferris. Oral History as told to Mary Ellen Reardon (2021).

Oral History interviews with Greg Post. Oral History as told to Mary Ellen Reardon (2019, 2020, 2021).

Oral History interviews with Donna Kowal. Oral History as told to Mary Ellen Reardon (2019, 2020, 2021).

Oral History interviews with Marilyn Rabenhorst. Oral History as told to Mary Ellen Reardon (2021).

Personal papers held by Ed Ferris. Viewed 2020.

Seven Springs Club Members Held a Meeting. (1927. May 28). *The Batavia Times*. Retrieved from: https://fultonhistory.com/Fulton.html.

Seven Springs Country Club. (1911, March 10). Meeting of Directors, SSCC files, Batavia, NY.

Seven Springs Country Club. (1917, July 11). Meeting of the Board of Directors, SSCC files, Batavia, NY.

Seven Springs Country Club. (1921, February 21). Meeting of the Board of Directors, SSCC files, Batavia, NY.

Seven Springs Country Club. (1921, April 10). Meeting of the Board of Directors, SSCC files, Batavia, NY.

Seven Springs Country Club. (1921, May). Meeting of the Board of Directors, SSCC files, Batavia, NY.

Seven Springs Country Club. (1923, July). Meeting of the Board of Directors, SSCC files, Batavia, NY.

Seven Springs Country Club. (1924, July). Meeting of the Board of Directors, Book held by Ed Ferris, Batavia, NY.

Seven Springs Country Club. (1924, August). Meeting of the Board of Directors, Book held by Ed Ferris, Batavia, NY.

Seven Springs Country Club. (1925, May). Meeting of the Board of Directors, Book held by Ed Ferris, Batavia, NY.

Seven Springs Country Club. (1926, January). Meeting of the Board of Directors, Book held by Ed Ferris, Batavia, NY.

Seven Springs Country Club. (1926, May). Meeting of the Board of Directors, Book held by Ed Ferris, Batavia, NY.

Seven Springs Country Club. (1926, July). Meeting of the Board of Directors, Book held by Ed Ferris, Batavia, NY.

Seven Springs Country Club. (1927, May). Annual Meeting of the Club, Book held by Ed Ferris, Batavia, NY.

Seven Springs Country Club. (1928, October). Meeting of the Board

of Directors, Book held by Ed Ferris, Batavia, NY.
Seven Springs Country Club. (1929, March). Meeting of the Board of Directors, Book held by Ed Ferris, Batavia, NY.
Seven Springs Country Club. (1929, April). Meeting of the Board of Directors, Book held by Ed Ferris, Batavia, NY.
Seven Springs Country Club. (1929, May). Meeting of the Board of Directors, Book held by Ed Ferris, Batavia, NY.
Seven Springs Country Club. (1929, July). Meeting of the Board of Directors, Book held by Ed Ferris, Batavia, NY.
Seven Springs Country Club. (1931, May). Meeting of the Board of Directors, Book held by Ed Ferris, Batavia, NY.
Seven Springs Country Club. (1932, May). Meeting of the Board of Directors, Book held by Ed Ferris, Batavia, NY.
Seven Springs Country Club. (2021, April 9). Meeting of the Board of Directors, SSCC files, Batavia, NY.
Seven Springs Record Book. (Oct 25, 1910-May 38, 2924). Record Book, SSCC Files, Batavia, NY
Unknown author. Brief history. Original copy held by Genesee County History Department. Retrieved: August 2021.
Very Personal. (1935, September 12). *The Times*, p 4. Retrieved from: https://fultonhistory.com/Fulton.html

EPILOGUE

Seven Springs has been a part of my life for 30 years and my home for nearly that long. It is my sincere hope that you have enjoyed reading this history of Seven Springs as much as I have enjoyed writing it.

CONTACT

For more information about Seven Springs, please send inquiries to sevenspringscountryclub@gmail.com

ABOUT THE AUTHOR

Maryellen Reardon

Mary Ellen Reardon lives in Western N.Y. with her husband and three sons. She is a Nurse and a passionate family genealogist. She enjoys researching and writing as well as being a part of the community in which she was raised.

She and her husband were introduced to Seven springs in 1991 and have spent the past 30 years living in the peace and beauty of its woods. The History of Seven Springs is a project a long time in the making to honor the place she loves so much.

When not researching or writing she is likely to be found at an ice rink cheering on her three favorite hockey players!

Made in United States
North Haven, CT
09 September 2023